Ninja Foodi Cookbook For Beginners

Quick, Easy, and Healthy Ninja Foodi Multi-Cooker Recipes for You and Your Partner

By Laurel Barnes

Table of Content

Introduction

When you buy a Ninja Foodi, it is essential to have a cookbook. Because it is a unique device, That why I am writing this book. First of all, congratulations! You made an excellent choice when you bought a Ninja Foodie! If you are still sitting at the fence, this cookbook is also for you! This cookbook introduces the different models, explains how to use your Ninja Foodi, briefly describes the cooking functions, and gives some tips. Then we start with the Ninja Foodi!

So this book is suitable for the working mom, Instant pot and vegetarian beginners, working professionals, and cooking lovers who want to learn cooking with ninja foodi.

This book aims to solve the problem of if you are going to cook some ninja foodi recipes, then get this book. It will guide you in an absolute way. A great learning book. Some important approaches provided. Recommended. This is such a great book and. Too simple; however, it gives you a great understanding. I am sure you will enjoy reading this book.

Ninja Foodi opens up a world of cooking options. It does not just make your favorite recipes easy, but also shorten the Preparation time significantly. I recommend you to prepare your dishes. Shift the boundaries of what your Ninja Foodi can do, and you will be happier in the long run

The following characteristics are used with the pressure cooking lid on. Pressure cooker: The pressure The dishes are simple, but also shorten the Preparation time significantly. I recommend you to prepare your dishes. Shift the boundaries of what your Ninja Foodi can do, and you will be happier in the long run

This book help reader the things that affect day-to-day life - such as your job, taking care of your family, getting errands done, etc. - can sometimes make it impossible for you to find the time to cook a decent dinner. An Air Fryer and this cookbook loaded with delicious recipes will help you cook healthy meals every day!

Try the ninja foodi recipes under various sections such as breakfast, lunch, side dishes, main dishes, snacks and appetizers, fish and seafood, poultry, meat, vegetable meals, and desserts.

If you are not sure what a Ninja Foodi is, or if you are not sure what features it offers, here is a brief description of how it works: A Foodi Ninja with Tender Crisp technology is an all-electric kitchen appliance Kitchen works. ,

Its two main features are the pressure cooker and the fryer, but it does a lot more as well. The following functions are available:

NINJA

The Following Characteristics Are Used With The Pressure Cooking Lid On.

Pressure cooker:

The pressure cooker function can be set to High or Low, and you can set the cooking time of the food to up to 4 hours. If you are using the Quick Cook feature, close the black valve on the top of the Foodi to make sure it closes tightly.

Steam: When using the steam regulator, there is no temperature control. You can set the time for up to 30 minutes.

Slow Cook: This function works as a Slow Cooker and can be set to Hi or Low. You can adjust the time up to 12 hours. When using this function, the black valve in the upper assembly should be vented and not sealed.

The following feature is used without a lid on the Ninja Foodi.

Sear / Sauté: This function has several temperature settings; Hi, Med-Hi, Med, Med-Low, and Low. You cannot set the time for this feature. It stays on until you turn it off.

The following features are used with the crisping lid on.

Air Crisp with Tender Crisp technology: The Air Crisp function provides temperature settings from 300 ° F to 400 ° F and allows you to change the periods up to 1 hour. F, and you can change the periods up to 4 hours.

Broil: The roasting function has no temperature setting; it is activated or deactivated. You can set the time for up to 30 minutes.

Bake Roast: The baking/roasting function has temperature settings from 250° F up to 400° F, and you can customize the duration up to 4 hours

Getting Started with the Ninja Foodi

Before first use:

After unpacking the Ninja Foodi, you want to wash the washable parts. I recommend washing the silicone ring (on the top basket), the basket, the basket, and the inner pot with the dishwasher.

Never place the lid of the pressure cooker or Ninja Foodi tray in the dishwasher. I read that many people clean the lid of their pressure cooker in the dishwasher, but I do not recommend it.

Before first use and after each use. I recommend to clean this by hand; a toothbrush works very well. Clogging protection protects the internal pressure valve against blockage.

If the internal valve is clogged, food may spurt out of the relief valve when the pressure is released. I've never noticed food or dirt in my close lid, but it's always a good idea to clean it.

You must also set up a condensate tray before first use. This does not affect the operation of Ninja Foodi, but it collects condensation that may form under pressure or steam during cooking. Be sure to remove and clean after each use. It is simple to skip, but I have heard of mildew if the water does not drain. You should only worry about it when cooking with the pressure cap. When using the soft, crisp lid, no condensation occurs.

Pressure Test:

Once you have your Ninja Foodi for the first time, familiarize yourself with it and make sure it works as expected. The easiest way is to do a pressure test. The pressure test is straightforward. Put three cups of water to the inner pot, attach the pressure cap, and rotate the black stopcock to seal. Select the push button, select up with the left indicator, and 3 minutes with the right indicator. Press Start.

You will see a bright rotating square indicating that the Ninja Foodi is heating up. It can take 8 to 10 minutes. The Ninja Foodi needs to heat the water to produce the steam required for the pressure. During this time, you may see steam coming out of the black valve and/or the red button on top of the lid. This is normal. If steam comes out of the lid, this is not normal. Stop the Ninja Foodi, turn the black valve to rinse, and let the steam escape.

Remove the lid and allow it to cool. The most common reason is that the seal is not placed correctly. Make sure that the silicone gasket is inserted in the grooves of the pressure cooker cover.

Ninja Foodi And Its Various Functions

Pressure cooker function: The pressure cooker is essentially a saucepan equipped with a sealed lid with a valve (the black valve that turns from the seal to the vent) for release the pressure, and a breather/button (the red button), pressure is on This article refers to an electric pressure cooker such as the Ninja Foodi: The quick cook function is an excellent way to speed up the cooking process. The food is usually prepared in 1/3 of the time; it would take on the stove or in the oven. For example, an entire chicken takes about 20 minutes per pound to be fried. Under pressure, it should take about 5 minutes per pound. In this entire chicken recipe with the instant pot, I went with 4 minutes per pound plus two additional minutes. In the end, and honestly, I do not think I need the extra additional minutes.

Steam function: I like all the functions of Ninja Foodi and find each of them useful, but the steam feature is my option to warm leftovers that are not cooked outdoors. I just put what I want to warm with aluminum foil on the lid of the aluminum molds and place it with 2 cups of water on the bottom of the grid (high or low position). I set the steam function for 5 to 10 minutes, depending on the density of the food I eat, and that's it! A perfectly roasted food that stores moisture without overcooking. The steam function differs from the quick-cooking function because steam can escape during cooking. It is an excellent option for vegetables, delicate fish, and rice. You can also remove the lid during cooking to control the food. However, be careful, and open it, because a lot of steam has accumulated, and it is hot.

Slow Cooking function: As if there were not enough applications for the Ninja Foodi, it even has a Slow Cooking function. You can set the temperature to high or low, and remember to set the black valve to air when you are cooking slowly. We want to release the accumulated steam. Although most of us love the speed of quick-cooking, the slow cooking function is undoubtedly useful. The other day I tried to decide for dinner and found that all my meat was frozen. Of course, I was able to cook frozen meat, but it was early in the day, and I decided to try a pork fillet in the slow cooker. I added the Ingredients, put them on top of it, and my pork and vegetable curry (I added them in the last hour) was ready on time for dinner. It was a dinner without hands and delicious.

Sear/Sauté function: I like this feature of Ninja Foodi and use it always. Now meat is no longer a warranty, as in a stainless steel pot, but I think the warranty is enough for what I use. You can use this setting at many different temperatures, although I tend to use the higher setting. It is ideal for frying vegetables before adding broth and other Ingredients to prepare soups or stews. Heat the milk to make home-made yogurt at Ninja Foodi.

Air Crisp Function: One of the main selling points of Ninja Foodi is the Air Crisp feature! It works very well, I have never had an air fryer in front of the Ninja Foodi, so I cannot compare an independent fryer with the Foodi, but I love this feature. One of the benefits of Ninja Foodi is that you can cook under pressure and brown or burn the meat with the fresh air function.

Bake/Roast function: The cooking/frying function of the Ninja Foodi works like a small convection oven. I did several tests with this feature because people said they burned their food when they used the cooking/frying feature. What I found is that the temperatures are accurate. If the temperature is set to 350 ° F, it is heated to 350 ° F. Why cook faster? The fan circulates the hot air. When cooking in a hot air oven, the food is faster. Sometimes this is great, and sometimes, as with bread and the densest foods, too much brown food may come out and remain uncooked in the middle. To remedy this, I suggest you lower the temperature by 10 ° C. Example: If your cornbread recipe requires a temperature of 425 ° F, set the cooking/frying function to 375 ° F and cook in the oven. Displayed temperature. Remember that you can lift the lid at any time to check the progress. Do not overdo it, as you release the heat each time you open the lid.

Broil Function: There is a difference between the cooking/frying function and the frying function. There! Heats more than 25 ° F as the cooking/frying function. Although you cannot set a temperature for the roast function, it will reach about 425 ° F after 15 minutes. I will certainly use this feature more intensively soon. I have not had time to do the tests on this topic yet.

Time and temp settings

You may need some adjustment, but you'll get great results if you know your Ninja Foodi. When experimenting, you may even find that you prefer other configurations. For example, you can specify that certain vegetables should not be cooked in steam mode but under pressure.

You can use the TEMP arrows to set the temperature up and down and then use the UP and DOWN arrow keys to select the cooking time of your food. Some Ninja Foodi cooking modes, such as the option to cook under pressure, activate the practical "keep warm" mode of the kitchen. When the cooking time has elapsed, the appliance beeps and automatically changes to the "Keep warm" setting.

Start a new timer to let you know how long your meal is resting. If the idea of using a slow cooker with no built-in presence will fill you with culinary worries, many online tips will help you achieve that tricky balance. And the temperature Starts small with simple recipes, but always make sure that the food, especially the meat, is well cooked.

Chapter 1 Meal Plans of 4 Weeks

1st Week Meal Plan

Days	Breakfast	Lunch	Dinner	Dessert
1	Breakfast Frittata	Bread-Crusted Salmon with Millet	Cauliflower Bites	Zeppole
2	Caramel Quinoa	Turkey Wings	Tomato-Rich Fish Stew	Figs Bites
3	Omelette	Brazil nuts Sweet Potatoes	Slow Cooked Sweet Potato Pork Chilli	Beetroots Peaches Cake Bites
4	Barley with Apples	Crispy Fried Salmon	Lamb, Cauliflower and Spicy Rice	Key Lime Pie
5	Blackberry Muffins	Garlic Turkey	Pinto Beans & Potatoes	Squash Cupcakes
6	Chocolate Millet	Fish Sticks	Garlic Beef Quinoa	Flax seeds cashew Bites
7	Greens Sauté	Broccoli, Potato & Spinach Curry	Artichoke Turkey	Pears Pie

2nd Week Meal Plan

Days	Breakfast	Lunch	Dinner	Dessert
1	Apple Basil Flatbread	Garlic Beef Quinoa	Baked Dijon Tuna	Squash Cupcakes
2	Quinoa Pudding	Jambalaya	Chicken and Wild Rice Soup	Pears Pie
3	Breakfast Hash	Brazil nuts Sweet Potatoes	Coconut Turkey	Flax seeds cashew Bites
4	Almond Butter Toast	Pinto Beans & Potatoes	Mahi Mahi and Coconut Stew	Beetroots Peaches Cake Bites
5	Spiced Nuts	Turkey Wings	Peanut butter Chicken	Figs Bites
6	Caramel Quinoa	Cauliflower Bites	Shredded Sweet Potato Cod Cakes	Zeppole
7	Chocolate Millet	Panko Lamb Bites	Curried Jackfruit	Peaches Bundt Cake

3rd Week Meal Plan

Days	Breakfast	Lunch	Dinner	Dessert
1	Breakfast Hash	Garbanzos Stew	Crumbed Chicken Tenderloins	Figs Bites
2	Squash Fries with Marinara Sauce	Shrimp and Eggplant Gumbo	Pinto Beans & Potatoes	Beetroots Peaches Cake Bites
3	Potato and Beetroots Latkes	Mushroom & Sweet Potato Chilli	Garlic Lamb with Risotto	Zeppole
4	Barley with Apples	Lamb, Cauliflower and Spicy Rice	Broccoli, Potato & Spinach Curry	Pears Pie
5	Chocolate Millet	Shredded Sweet Potato Cod Cakes	Lamb Fingers	Peaches Bundt Cake
6	Spiced Nuts	Jambalaya	kidney beans Curry	Flax seeds cashew Bites
7	Quinoa Pudding	Pork Lettuce Wraps	Crispy Fried Salmon	Squash Cupcakes

4Th Week Meal Plan

Days	Breakfast	Lunch	Dinner	Dessert
1	Omelette	Braised Red wine Chicken	Bread-Crusted Salmon with Millet	Peaches Bundt Cake
2	Banana Bread	Beef Grains, Greens Bowl	Fish Stew	Pears Pie
3	Breakfast Hash	Coconut Turkey	Whole Roasted Broccoli	Flax seeds cashew Bites
4	Quinoa Pudding	Shrimp and Eggplant Gumbo	Sweet, Sticky and Spicy Chicken	Beetroots Peaches Cake Bites
5	Barley with Apples	Garlic Beef Quinoa	Mushroom & Sweet Potato Chilli	Squash Cupcakes
6	Breakfast Frittata	Turkey Wings	Garbanzos Stew	Zeppole
7	Blackberry Muffins	Garlic Lamb with Risotto	Cauliflower Bites	Figs Bites

Chapter 2 Breakfast and Brunch

Breakfast Frittata

(Prep Time: 15 min |Cooking Time: 20 min | serve: 2)

Ingredients

- 1 teaspoon avocado oil
- ½ medium celery ,
- ¼ cup mushrooms, thinly sliced
- 4 eggs
- 1/2 cup Sour cream
- ¼ tablespoon fresh basil, minced
- 1/8 cup shredded goat cheese, divided
- 1/4 teaspoon kosher salt
- 1/4 teaspoon freshly ground black pepper
- ¼ cup water

Preparation

1. Select SEAR/SAUTÉ and set to High. Select START/STOP to begin. Add avocado oil and allow to preheat for 5 minutes.
2. After 5 minutes, add celery and cook until softened, about 5 minutes. Then add mushrooms. Cook, stirring often, until liquid has evaporated.
3. While mushrooms are cooking, whisk together the eggs, sour cream , and basil in a large bowl. Stir in goat cheese, salt, and pepper.
4. Once liquid has evaporated, remove mushrooms and leeks from the pot and stir into the egg mixture.
5. Add water to the pot. Place the Ninja multi-purpose pan on the reversible rack, making sure rack is in the lower position. Place rack with pan in pot.
6. Close the crisping lid. Preheat the unit by selecting BROIL and setting time to 5 minutes. Select START/STOP to begin.
7. When unit is preheated, open the crisping lid and generously spray the pan with cooking spray. Pour egg mixture into the pan.
8. Assemble the pressure lid, making sure the pressure release valve is in the SEAL position. Select PRESSURE and set to HIGH. Set time to 10 minutes. Select START/STOP to begin.

9. When pressure cooking is complete, allow the pressure to release naturally for 10 minutes. After 10 minutes, quick release the remaining pressure by moving the pressure release valve to the VENT position. Carefully remove lid when unit has finished releasing pressure.
10. Pat the surface of the frittata with a paper towel to remove excess moisture. Sprinkle goat cheese on top. Close the crisping lid, select BROIL, and set time to 7 minutes. Select START/STOP to begin.
11. When cooking is complete, frittata is ready to serve

Nutrition Facts

Calories 132, Total Fat 10.9g, Saturated Fat 5.4g, Cholesterol 177mg, Sodium 232mg, Total Carbohydrate 2g, Dietary Fiber 0.2g, Total Sugars 0.6g, Protein 6.9g

Omelette

(Prep Time: 10 min |Cooking Time: 35 min | serve: 2)

Ingredients

- 4 eggs
- ¼ cup coconut milk
- Kosher salt and pepper, to taste
- ½ cup shredded mozzarella cheese
- ¼ cup tofu, diced
- ¼ cup red bell pepper, diced
- ¼ cup green bell pepper, diced
- ¼ cup fresh parsley, diced

Preparation

1. Close crisping lid. Preheat the unit by selecting BAKE/ROAST, setting the temperature to 315°F, and setting the time to 5 minutes. Select START/STOP to begin.
2. Meanwhile, in a medium bowl, whisk together eggs, coconut milk, salt, and pepper. Then add remaining Ingredients and stir to combine.
3. Generously grease the bottom of the Ninja multi-purpose pan with cooking spray. Pour egg mixture into pan and place pan on reversible rack, making sure rack is in the lower position.
4. Once unit is preheated, place rack with pan in pot. Close crisping lid. Select BAKE/ROAST, set temperature to 315°F, and set time to 35 minutes. Select START/STOP to begin.
5. When cooking is complete, omelette is ready to serve.

Nutrition Facts

Calories 127, Total Fat 9.3g, Saturated Fat 5.1g, Cholesterol 166mg, Sodium 239mg, Total Carbohydrate 3.4g, Dietary Fiber 1.1g, Total Sugars 1.9g, Protein 8.6g

Barley with Apples

(Prep Time: 05 min |Cooking Time: 15 min | serve: 2)

Ingredients

- 1 cup barley
- 3 cups water
- 1-2 apples, cored, cut in quarters, sliced in 1/2-inch pieces
- ¼ cup blueberries
- ½ teaspoon ground nutmeg
- ¼ cup coconut sugar
- ½ tablespoon butter

Preparation

1. Place barley, water, apples, raisins, and nutmeg into the pot. Assemble pressure lid, making sure the pressure release valve is in the SEAL position.
2. Select PRESSURE and set to HIGH. Set time to 10 minutes. Select START/STOP to begin.
3. When pressure cooking is complete, natural release pressure for 10 minutes, then quick release any remaining pressure by turning the pressure release valve to the VENT position. Carefully remove lid when unit has finished releasing pressure.
4. Select SEAR/SAUTÉ and set to MEDIUM-HIGH. Select START/STOP to begin.
5. Add coconut sugar and butter to pot. Stir for 3 to 4 minutes, or until desired consistency is reached. Serve immediately.

Nutrition Facts

Calories 217, Total Fat 2.7g, Saturated Fat 1.2g, Cholesterol 4mg, Sodium 24mg, Total Carbohydrate 44.1g, Dietary Fiber 9.6g, Total Sugars 7.2g, Protein 6.1g

Caramel Quinoa

(Prep Time: 05 min |Cooking Time: 10 min | serve: 2)

Ingredients

- 1 cup quinoa
- 1 1/2 cups water
- ½ teaspoon sea salt
- 1 cup applesauce
- ¼ cup butter
- ½ cup coconut sugar
- ¼ cup coconut cream

Preparation

1. In the inner pot of the Ninja Foodi, combine 1 cup of barley with water. Add salt and applesauce. Stir.
2. Combine butter and coconut sugar in a 6" cake pan and cover with foil. Place the rack in the high position and put the cake pan on top.
3. Put the pressure lid on and turn the valve to seal. Set the pressure on LOW for 10 minutes. When the time is up, allow to natural release for 7 minutes, then release the remaining pressure.
4. Whisk the coconut sugar and butter until it is combined. Pour into the barley and stir.
5. Serve with coconut cream if desired. Enjoy!

Nutrition Facts

Calories 331, Total Fat 17.7g, Saturated Fat 10.8g, Cholesterol 31mg, Sodium 329mg, Total Carbohydrate 37.4g, Dietary Fiber 4g, Total Sugars 6.7g, Protein 6.7g

Chocolate Millet

(Prep Time: 05 min |Cooking Time: 05 min | serve: 2)

Ingredients

- 1 cup millet
- 4 cups coconut milk
- ½ cup chocolate chips
- ¼ cup brown sugar

Preparation

1. Spray the inside of your oven safe dish with non-stick spray.
2. Add millet and coconut milk and brown sugar into your bowl and stir. Add 1.5 c water into your pot and lower your trivet down with your filled bowl on top.
3. Put pressure cooker lid on (one that isn't attached) and close steam valve.
4. Set for pressure, high, for 5 minutes.
5. Do a quick release, stir, and serve with chocolate chips on top!

Nutrition Facts

Calories 538, Total Fat 33.8g, Saturated Fat 27.9g, Cholesterol 2mg, Sodium 30mg, Total Carbohydrate 53.8g, Dietary Fiber 7.3g, Total Sugars 13.8g, Protein 9.1g

Blackberry Muffins

(Prep Time: 05 min |Cooking Time: 05 min | serve: 2)

Ingredients

- ½ cup coconut flour
- ½ teaspoon baking powder
- ¼ teaspoon baking soda
- ¼ teaspoon salt
- 2 teaspoons maple syrup
- ¾ cup buttermilk
- 1 tablespoon olive oil
- 1 egg
- 3 tablespoons canned blackberries, drained
- Cooking spray
- 1 ½ cups hot water

Preparation

1. Stir coconut flour, baking powder, baking soda, salt, and maple syrup in bowl.
2. Beat buttermilk, oil, and egg in another bowl.
3. Add buttermilk mixture to flour mixture and stir just until combined. Stir in blueberries.
4. Spray 6-cup muffin pan with cooking spray. Spoon batter into muffin-pan cups.
5. Pour water into pot. Place roasting rack into pot. Place pan on rack.
6. Set OVEN to 350 °F for 25 minutes. Cover and cook until wooden pick inserted in centres comes out clean.

Nutrition Facts

Calories 73, Total Fat 4.4g, Saturated Fat 1.3g, Cholesterol 34mg, Sodium 239mg, Total Carbohydrate 6g, Dietary Fiber 1.3g, Total Sugars 3.9g, Protein 2.8g

Breakfast Hash

(Prep Time: 05 min |Cooking Time: 05 min | serve: 2)

Ingredients

- ½ cup sweet potatoes, peeled, cut in 1/2-inch pieces
- 1/8 cup precooked Spanish chorizo, cut in 1/2-inch pieces
- ½ small onion, peeled, cut in 1/2-inch pieces
- ¼ cup mixed vegetables like carrots, green beans, corn
- 1 tablespoon avocado oil
- ½ teaspoon paprika
- ½ teaspoon salt

Preparation

1. Place Sweet potatoes, Spanish chorizo, onion, and frozen vegetables in a large bowl. Add avocado, paprika and salt. Toss Ingredients to coat.
2. Place Ingredients on Ninja Sheet Pan, spreading out evenly.
3. Select BAKE, set temperature to 400°F, and set time to 20 minutes. Press START/PAUSE to begin preheating.
4. When unit has preheated, place pan in oven. After 10 minutes, remove pan and mix Ingredients with a wooden spoon or spatula. Return pan to oven and cook for 10 more minutes.
5. When cooking is complete, remove pan from oven and cool for 5 minutes before serving.

Nutrition Facts

Calories 77, Total Fat 1.1g, Saturated Fat 0.2g, Cholesterol 0mg, Sodium 594mg, Total Carbohydrate 15.8g, Dietary Fiber 3.4g, Total Sugars 1.7g, Protein 1.6g

Banana Bread

(Prep Time: 15 min |Cooking Time: 40 min | serve: 2)

Ingredients

- 2 cups coconut flour
- 1 teaspoon baking soda
- 1/4 teaspoon kosher salt
- 2 tablespoon coconut oil
- ¼ cup maple syrup
- 2 eggs, beaten
- 3 medium ripe bananas, mashed

Preparation

1. Close crisping lid. Preheat the unit by selecting BAKE/ROAST, setting the temperature to 325°F, and setting the time to 5 minutes. Select START/STOP to begin.
2. Meanwhile, in a bowl, stir together coconut flour, baking soda, and salt.
3. In a separate bowl, beat together coconut oil and maple syrup. Add eggs and bananas and stir to combine.
4. Slowly add dry mixture to wet mixture, stirring until just combined.
5. Grease the Ninja loaf pan (or an 8-inch baking pan) and add batter to pan.
6. Once unit has preheated, place pan on reversible rack, making sure rack is in the lower position. Close crisping lid. Select BAKE/ROAST, set temperature to 325°F, and set time to 40 minutes. Select START/STOP to begin.
7. When cooking is complete, remove pan from pot and place on a cooling rack. Allow bread to cool 30 minutes before serving.

Nutrition Facts

Calories 651, Total Fat 66.3g, Saturated Fat 41.6g, Cholesterol 0mg, Sodium 24mg, Total Carbohydrate 17.3g, Dietary Fiber 10.5g, Total Sugars 5g, Protein 6.5g

Almond Butter Toast

(Prep Time: 10 min |Cooking Time: 00 min | serve: 2)

Ingredients

- 2 slices Tempeh, cooked, cooled
- 2 tablespoons almond butter
- ½ tablespoon tomato sauce
- ½ tablespoon fresh lime juice
- 1/8 teaspoon salt
- 1/8 teaspoon ground pepper
- 2 slices browned bread, toasted

Preparation

1. Place the Total Crushing & Power Chopping Blade into the Jar, then add cooked Tempeh.
2. Pulse 3 times, then transfer chopped bacon to a small bowl.
3. Add almond butter, tomato sauce, lime juice, salt, and pepper to the jar. Pulse 7 times, then run continuously for 20 seconds.
4. Top each slice of toasted bread with approximately 2 tablespoons almond butter spread and chopped tempeh.

Nutrition Facts

Calories232, Total Fat 12.1g, Saturated Fat 1.4g, Cholesterol 0mg, Sodium 320mg, Total Carbohydrate 25.2g, Dietary Fiber 3.7g,, Total Sugars 7.1g, Protein 9.4g

Quinoa Pudding

(Prep Time: 05 min |Cooking Time: 05 min | serve: 2)

Ingredients

- ½ cup quinoa
- 2 cups coconut milk, cold, divided
- 1/8 cup maple syrup
- 2 strips lime zest
- 1 cinnamon sticks
- 1/8 teaspoon kosher salt
- 1/2 cup heavy cream
- Ground nutmeg, for garnish

Preparation

1. Place quinoa, 1-1/2 cups coconut milk, maple syrup, lime zest, cinnamon sticks, and salt into the pot. Stir to combine.
2. Assemble pressure lid, making sure the pressure release valve is in the SEAL position. Select PRESSURE and set to HIGH. Set time to 2 minutes. Select START/STOP to begin.
3. When pressure cooking is complete, allow pressure to release naturally for 10 minutes. After 10 minutes, quick release any remaining pressure by moving the pressure release valve to the VENT position. Carefully remove lid when unit has finished releasing pressure.
4. Add heavy cream to the pot and stir to incorporate.
5. Select SEAR/SAUTÉ and set to MED. Select START/STOP to begin. Allow to simmer for 5 minutes, stirring frequently.
6. Carefully remove pot to a heat-safe surface. Stir in the remaining milk and allow to cool for 15 minutes.
7. Serve warm after 15 minutes, or cool to room temperature then refrigerate and serve cold, garnished with ground nutmeg

Nutrition Facts

Calories 543, Total Fat 37.9g, Saturated Fat 28.6g, Cholesterol 41mg, Sodium 178mg, Total Carbohydrate 45.5g, Dietary Fiber 3.6g, Total Sugars 11.8g, Protein 9g

Chapter 3 Vegan and Vegetable

Garbanzos Stew

(Prep Time: 15 min |Cooking Time: 15 min | serve: 2)

Ingredients

- 1 cup Garbanzos, drained
- ½ cup sweet potatoes, peeled and cut into 1inch pieces
- 1 large beets, peeled and sliced
- 1storks leek, sliced
- ½ onion
- ½ cup chopped tomatoes
- 1 bay leaves
- 1 cup vegetable broth
- 1 tablespoon tomato puree
- 1 tablespoon avocado oil
- ½ teaspoon salt

Preparation

1. Put all the Ingredients into the Foodi Ninja cooking pot and mix well
2. Assemble the pressure lid, close and turn the valve to SEAL
3. Select the pressure function
4. Put 8 minutes on the timer and press start
5. Once the time is done, carefully move the valve to VENT (prepare for the most delicious smell to come into your kitchen)
6. When all the steam has been released, open the lid, stir and it's ready. Serve and enjoy!

Nutrition Facts

Calories 275, Total Fat 4g, Saturated Fat 0.9g, Cholesterol 0mg, Sodium 1654mg, Total Carbohydrate 49.3g, Dietary Fiber 4.7g, Total Sugars 14.3g, Protein 11.8g

Cauliflower Bites

(Prep Time: 20 min |Cooking Time: 10 min | serve: 2)

Ingredients

- 1 large head of Cauliflower (cut into florets)
- ½ cup coconut milk
- 1/8 cup coconut flour
- 2 tablespoons corn starch
- Juice from 1/4 lime
- 1 teaspoon soy sauce
- Pinch of salt
- ½ cup crushed cornflakes
- 1 tablespoon Greek yogurt
- Chopped basil

Preparation

1. Combine coconut flour, corn starch, coconut milk, salt, lime juice and soy sauce
2. crushed cornflakes into a bowl, and then dip each cauliflower floret into the batter before coating thoroughly with cornflakes
3. Add to your Ninja Foodi, and cook on air crisp setting at 200C for 10 minutes
4. Serve with Greek yogurt and chopped basil

Nutrition Facts

Calories 230, Total Fat 8.6g, Saturated Fat 7.2g, Cholesterol 3mg, Sodium 286mg, Total Carbohydrate 31.5g, Dietary Fiber 7.2g, Total Sugars 8.9g, Protein 11.2g

Whole Roasted Broccoli

(Prep Time: 25 min |Cooking Time: 10 min | serve: 2)

Ingredients

- ½ cup water
- 1 head Broccoli
- 2 tablespoons coconut oil
- 1 teaspoon garlic powder
- ½ teaspoon dried chilli flakes
- 2 tablespoons grated goat cheese

For Serving

- ½ tablespoon fresh basil, chopped
- Fresh lemon wedges

Preparation

1. Place water and Cook & Crisp Basket into the pot.
2. Remove the leaves from broccoli. With a knife, trim the stalk of the broccoli and cut an X into the head, slicing about halfway down. Place the broccoli into the basket.
3. Assemble the pressure lid, making sure the pressure release valve is in the SEAL position. Select PRESSURE and set to LOW. Set time to 3 minutes. Select START/STOP to begin.
4. In a small bowl, stir together the coconut oil, garlic powder, and dried chilli flakes.
5. When pressure cooking is complete, quick release the pressure by moving the pressure release valve to the VENT position.
6. Spread the coconut oil mixture evenly over the broccoli, placing some of it into the centre of the broccoli. Sprinkle goat cheese evenly over the broccoli.
7. Close the crisping lid. Select AIR CRISP, set temperature to 180°C, and set time to 10 minutes. Select START/STOP to begin.
8. When cooking is complete, transfer the broccoli to a serving platter using a large spatula. Garnish with fresh parsley and lemon wedges.

Nutrition Facts

Calories 269, Total Fat 24g, Saturated Fat 18.7g, Cholesterol 30mg, Sodium 115mg, Total Carbohydrate 5.2g, Dietary Fiber 1.7g, Total Sugars 1.7g, Protein 10.3g

Mushroom & Sweet Potato Chilli

(Prep Time: 20 min |Cooking Time: 10 min | serve: 2)

Ingredients

- 1tablespoon coconut oil
- 1 Sweet potatoes, chopped into small cubes
- ¼ cup mushrooms
- 4 spring onions, chopped
- 1 cup tinned tomatoes
- ½ cup tinned pinto beans, drained
- ¼ cup sweetcorn
- 1 teaspoon chilli powder
- ½ teaspoon cumin
- ¼ teaspoon garlic powder
- ¼ teaspoon black pepper
- ¼ teaspoon oregano
- ½ teaspoon salt
- ¼ cup walnuts, for serving

Preparation

1. Select SEAR/SAUTÉ and set to HIGH, to preheat for 2 minutes
2. Add the coconut oil. After a few seconds, add the spring onions and sweet potatoes. When the sweet potatoes are starting to brown after about 3 minutes, add in the mushrooms and salt
3. Add in all spices and herbs and stir well for 1 minute
4. Press START/STOP to cancel SEAR/SAUTÉ. Pour in the tinned tomatoes, pinto beans and sweetcorn. Stir well, then put the pressure lid on, ensuring the pressure release valve is in the SEAL position
5. Select PRESSURE and set to HIGH for 3 minutes. Select START/STOP to begin
6. After 3 minutes, carefully move the pressure release valve to the VENT position to quick release the pressure. When all pressure has been released, remove the lid
7. Serve with a sprinkle of walnuts

Nutrition Facts

Calories 429, Total Fat 13.2g, Saturated Fat 2.7g, Cholesterol 0mg, Sodium 608mg, Total Carbohydrate 64.1g, Dietary Fiber 15g, Total Sugars 5.5g, Protein 17.9g

Brazil Nuts Sweet Potatoes

(Prep Time: 20 min |Cooking Time: 05 min | serve: 2)

Ingredients

- 1 tablespoon butter
- 2 medium Sweet potatoes, peeled and sliced into thin slices
- 1 green chillies, split in the middle and de-seeded
- 1-1/2 teaspoon cumin seeds
- 2 tablespoons crushed Brazil nuts
- Salt to taste
- Basil to garnish

Preparation

1. Put the Foodi on the Sauté/Sear settings with the temperature set to Medium. Press Start/Stop to begin
2. Wait for 5 minutes for it to heat up and then put in the butter and wait for it to splutter
3. Throw in the chillies and fry until they splutter and the butter is infused with the chillies
4. Add in the crushed brazil nuts and lightly fry them for a minute. Add in the cumin seeds and fry for 30 seconds
5. Put in the Sweet potatoes and salt, and stir until all Ingredients are mixed nicely
6. Assemble the pressure cooker lid and set pressure release valve to Vent
7. Monitor for 4 minutes and then switch off the Foodi
8. Open the lid after 5 minutes and garnish with basil

Nutrition Facts

Calories 251, Total Fat 16.7g, Saturated Fat 8.2g, Cholesterol 0mg, Sodium 114mg, Total Carbohydrate 24.4g, Dietary Fiber 4.2g, Total Sugars 0.9g, Protein 3.4g

Pinto Beans & Potatoes

(Prep Time: 20 min |Cooking Time: 4 hr | serve: 2)

Ingredients

- ½ cup pinto beans
- 1 carrots chopped
- 1 small potato, cut into chunks
- ½ red bell pepper
- 1 small red onion
- 1 fresh chilli
- ½ teaspoon coriander
- ½ teaspoon cumin
- ½ teaspoon chilli flakes
- ½ teaspoon garlic powder
- 1 teaspoon ginger powder
- ½ teaspoon turmeric
- ½ teaspoon curry powder
- 1 teaspoon Garam masala
- 1 cup almond milk
- ½ cup vegetable stock

Preparation

1. Chop all the vegetables and turn on your Ninja Foodi on to the slow cooker setting
2. Add all the Ingredients except the almond milk into the pot. Add a little more water if needed to cover all Ingredients
3. Place the lid on the slow cooker and turn on 'HI' for 4 hours
4. Once the slow cooking is complete, add the almond milk to the pot and stir
5. Put the Foodi on the 'Keep Warm' setting for about 15 minutes to let the almond milk heat

Nutrition Facts

Calories 391, Total Fat 8.6g, Saturated Fat 2.7g, Cholesterol 2mg, Sodium 58mg, Total Carbohydrate 65.3g, Dietary Fiber 12.9g, Total Sugars 14.6g, Protein 15.5g

Broccoli, Potato & Spinach Curry

(Prep Time: 20 min |Cooking Time: 10 min | serve: 2)

Ingredients

- ¼ broccoli, florets separated
- ¼ cup Spinach
- ½ potato, diced
- ½ cup pinto beans, drained
- 1 cup chopped tomatoes
- 1 cup coconut milk
- 1 teaspoon garlic powder
- 1 teaspoon paprika
- 1 teaspoon ginger powder
- 1 teaspoon cumin
- 1 tablespoon onion
- 1 teaspoon turmeric
- 1 teaspoon cinnamon
- Dash of salt

Preparation

1. Place all the Ingredients into Ninja Foodi
2. Stir all the Ingredients together to make sure that spices and vegetables are distributed evenly throughout. Curry should become an orange colour once everything is mixed
3. Select PRESSURE and set to HIGH. Set the time to 3 minutes and press the START/STOP button to begin
4. When the pressure cooking is complete, carefully quick release the pressure by turning the pressure release valve to the VENT position. Carefully remove the lid when the unit has finished releasing pressure
5. Once curry is done, use a spoon or ladle to place curry into bowls. If consistency is too watery, add a tsp at a time of corn-starch and mix until fully dissolved at desired consistency

Nutrition Facts

Calories 521, Total Fat 30g, Saturated Fat 25.6g, Cholesterol 0mg, Sodium 118mg, Total Carbohydrate 53.5g, Dietary Fiber 14.2g, Total Sugars 8.7g, Protein 16g

kidney Beans Curry

(Prep Time: 20 min |Cooking Time: 15 min | serve: 2)

Ingredients

- ½ cup kidney beans, washed and soaked for about eight an hour
- 1 onions, chopped
- ½ tablespoon ginger garlic paste
- ½ cup chopped tomatoes
- 2 green chillies, finely chopped
- 1 teaspoon cumin seeds
- 1 teaspoon turmeric
- 2 cups vegetable stock
- Salt, to taste
- Mint, to garnish

Preparation

1. Select SEAR/SAUTÉ and set the temperature to MEDIUM. Select START/STOP to begin.
2. Allow to preheat for 5 minutes, then add the coconut oil and wait for it to splutter.
3. Add the onions and chillies. Stir until the onions are soft.
4. Add the cumin seeds. When they start to splutter, add the chopped tomatoes and the ginger garlic paste.
5. Add the turmeric and salt. Fry the mixture until you see the oil separate.
6. Add in the kidney beans and mix well.
7. Add the vegetable stock. Assemble the Pressure Lid, making sure the pressure release valve is in the SEAL position. Select PRESSURE and set the temperature to HIGH. Set time to 15 minutes and select START/STOP to begin.
8. When cooking is complete, quick release the pressure by turning the valve to the VENT position.
9. Garnish with mint and serve.

Nutrition Facts

Calories 212, Total Fat 1.4g, Saturated Fat 0.1g, Cholesterol 0mg, Sodium 195mg, Total Carbohydrate 39.3g, Dietary Fiber 10.4g, Total Sugars 5.7g, Protein 12.5g

Curried Jackfruit

(Prep Time: 20 min |Cooking Time: 15 min | serve: 2)

Ingredients

- 1 tablespoon vegetable oil, divided, plus more as needed
- ½ cup jackfruit, cut into cubes
- ½ teaspoon salt, divided
- 1 small onions, peeled, thinly sliced
- ½ cup potato, peeled, cut into small cubes
- 1 teaspoon garlic powder
- 1 cup soy milk
- 1 teaspoon curry powder
- ½ tablespoon fresh coriander leaves, stems removed, chopped
- 1 tablespoon roasted walnuts, chopped
- Juice of 1 lime

Preparation

1. Select SEAR/SAUTÉ on your Foodi and set to HI. Select START/STOP to begin. Allow to preheat for 5 minutes
2. After 5 minutes, add vegetable oil. Once the vegetable oil begins to simmer, add the jackfruits and season with ½ teaspoon salt. Sear for about 2 minutes on each side, or until browned. Remove to a separate bowl and cover to keep warm
3. Add the remaining vegetable oil to the pot along with onions, potato, and salt to taste. Sauté for 2 minutes, or until the onions are translucent. Add garlic and cook, stirring frequently, for 30 seconds
4. Select START/STOP to turn off SEAR/SAUTÉ, then add the soy milk and curry powder. Assemble the pressure lid, making sure the pressure release valve is in the SEAL position
5. Select PRESSURE and set to HIGH. Set the time to 3 minutes and press the START/STOP button to begin
6. While the sauce is cooking, stir together chopped walnuts and lime juice in a small bowl.
7. When the pressure cooking is complete, carefully quick release the pressure by turning the pressure release valve to the VENT position. Carefully remove the lid when the unit has finished releasing pressure
8. Add the cooked jackfruits to the pot with the sauce. Using a spoon, sprinkle peanut and lime mixture on top of jackfruits, spreading as evenly as possible
9. Close the crisping lid. Select GRILL and set the time to 5 minutes. Press START/STOP to begin.

Nutrition Facts

Calories 233, Total Fat 11.5g, Saturated Fat 1.9g, Cholesterol 0mg, Sodium 650mg, Total Carbohydrate 28.3g, Dietary Fiber 3.5g, Total Sugars 7.4g, Protein 7g

Mixed Bean Chilli

(Prep Time: 10 min |Cooking Time: 15 min | serve: 2)

Ingredients

- 1 small onion, chopped
- 1 teaspoon garlic powder
- 1 sticks leek, chopped
- ½ red pepper, sliced
- 1 teaspoon red chilli powder
- 1 teaspoon cumin
- 1 cup chopped tomatoes
- 1 cup mixed beans, drained
- 1 tablespoon tomato puree
- 1 tablespoon coconut oil

Preparation

1. Select SEAR / SAUTE and set to high on your Ninja Kitchen Foodi. After 5 minutes add ½ tablespoon coconut oil, onion and garlic and cook for 5 minutes, stirring occasionally.
2. Add the leek, peppers and spices and continue cooking for 5 minutes.
3. Add the chopped tomatoes, beans, and tomato puree and stir well to combine. Place pressure lid on, select PRESSURE and set to LOW for 15 minutes.

Nutrition Facts

Calories 374, Total Fat 12.7g, Saturated Fat 6g, Cholesterol 0mg, Sodium 995mg, Total Carbohydrate 38g, Dietary Fiber 27.5g, Total Sugars 11.4g, Protein 13.9g

Chapter 4 Fish and Seafood

Bread-Crusted Salmon with Millet

(Prep Time: 10 min |Cooking Time: 25 min | serve: 2)

Ingredients

- ½ cup millet
- 1teaspoon salt, divided
- 1 cups water
- ½ cup bread crumbs
- 2 tablespoons coconut oil, melted
- 1/8 cup fresh basil, minced
- Zest and juice of 1 orange
- 2 salmon fillets
- ½ cup broccoli

Preparation

1. Place the millet, ¼ teaspoon salt, and water into the pot.
2. Assemble pressure lid, making sure the pressure release valve is in the SEAL position. Select PRESSURE and set to high (HI). Set time to 2 minutes. Select START/STOP to begin.
3. While millet is cooking, in a bowl, stir together the bread crumbs with coconut oil, basil, orange zest and juice, and ¼ teaspoon salt. Press bread mixture evenly onto the top of each salmon fillet.
4. When pressure cooking is complete, quick release the pressure by moving the pressure release valve to the VENT position. Carefully remove lid when unit has finished releasing pressure.
5. Toss the asparagus with coconut oil and 1 teaspoon salt. Lay broccoli evenly on top of millet.
6. Place the reversible rack in the pot over the millet and broccoli, making sure it is in the higher position. Place the cod fillets on the rack, breading side up.
7. Close the crisping lid. Select BAKE/ROAST, set the temperature to A 350°F, and set the time to 12 minutes. Select START/STOP to begin. Cook for up to an additional 2 minutes if necessary.
8. Cooking is complete when internal temperature reaches 145°F. Serve salmon with millet and broccoli.

Nutrition Facts

Calories 345, Total Fat 14.2g, Saturated Fat 7g, Cholesterol 39mg, Sodium 726mg, Total Carbohydrate 33.1g, Dietary Fiber 3.8g, Total Sugars 4g, Protein 22.5g

Fish Sticks

(Prep Time: 15 min |Cooking Time: 15 min | serve: 2)

Ingredients

- 1 cod fillets (4 ounces)
- ¼ cup coconut flour
- 1 large eggs, beaten
- ¼ cup panko bread crumbs
- ¼ teaspoon kosher salt

Preparation

1. Place coconut flour in a shallow bowl. Add eggs to another bowl. Combine panko and salt in a third bowl.
2. Working in small batches, dredge cod in flour. Tap off excess, then coat in egg. Then coat evenly with panko bread crumbs.
3. Insert crisper plate in basket. Preheat unit by selecting AIR FRY, setting the temperature to 390°F, and setting the time to 3 minutes. Select START/PAUSE to begin.
4. After 3 minutes, place 8 fish sticks on crisper plate; insert basket in unit.
5. Select AIR FRY, set temperature to 390°F, and set time to 12 minutes. Select START/PAUSE to begin.
6. Halfway through cooking, select START/PAUSE to pause cooking. Remove basket from unit and flip fish sticks. Reinsert basket and select START/PAUSE to resume cooking.
7. When cooking is complete, remove fish sticks from crisping plate. Squeeze lemon wedges over them and serve immediately with tartar sauce or ketchup.

Nutrition Facts

Calories 191, Total Fat 4.2g, Saturated Fat 1.3g, Cholesterol 143mg, Sodium 498mg, Total Carbohydrate 10.9g, Dietary Fiber 1.2g, Total Sugars 1.2g, Protein 25.8g

Baked Dijon Tuna

(Prep Time: 20 min |Cooking Time: 15 min | serve: 2)

Ingredients

- 1 tablespoon coconut oil, melted
- 1-1/2 tablespoons Dijon mustard
- 1 tablespoon maple syrup
- 1/8 cup dry bread crumbs
- 1/8 cup finely chopped walnuts
- 2 teaspoons chopped fresh basil
- 2 (4 ounce) fillets tuna
- Salt and pepper to taste
- 1 lemon, for garnish

Preparation

1. Close crisping lid. Preheat the unit by selecting BAKE/ROAST, setting the temperature to 315°F, and setting the time to 5 minutes. Select START/STOP to begin.
2. In a small bowl, stir together coconut oil, mustard, and maple syrup. Set aside. In another bowl, mix together bread crumbs, walnuts, and basil.
3. Brush each tuna fillet lightly with maple mustard mixture, and sprinkle the tops of the fillets with the bread crumb mixture.
4. Once unit is preheated, place rack with pan in pot. Close crisping lid. Select BAKE/ROAST, set temperature to 315°F, and set time to 25 minutes. Select START/STOP to begin.
5. When cooking is complete, Season with salt and pepper, and garnish with a wedge of lemon.

Nutrition Facts

Calories 268, Total Fat 20.9g, Saturated Fat 6.2g, Cholesterol 0mg, Sodium 139mg, Total Carbohydrate 12.8g, Dietary Fiber 1.1g, Total Sugars 6.5g, Protein 9.1g

Fish Stew

(Prep Time: 20 min |Cooking Time: 15 min | serve: 2)

Ingredients

- 1/8 cup avocado oil
- 2 stalks green onion
- 1/4 onion, diced
- 1-1/2 beetroots, diced
- 1 teaspoon garlic powder
- 2 tomatoes
- 2 1/2 cups water
- 1 (8 ounce) bottle clam juice
- 1/4 cup sherry
- 1/2 teaspoon red pepper flakes
- Salt and pepper to taste
- 1/2 bunch parsley
- 1/2 pound medium shrimp - peeled and deveined
- 1/2 pound white fish, cut into small chunks

Preparation

1. Heat the oil in a large pot over medium heat. Mix in the celery, onion, carrots, and garlic. Cook and stir until onion is tender. Stir in the tomatoes, water, wine, clam juice, and sherry. Dissolve bouillon cubes in the stew, and season with red pepper, salt, and pepper. Bring to a boil, reduce heat to low, and simmer 1 hour.
2. Mix the cilantro, shrimp, and fish into the stew. Continue cooking 5 minutes, or until shrimp is opaque and fish is easily flaked. Remove from heat, and allow to sit 10 minutes before serving
3. Select SEAR/SAUTÉ and set to HIGH. Select START/STOP to begin. Allow to preheat for 5 minutes.
4. After 5 minutes, add avocado oil, Mix in the green onion, onion, beets, and garlic powder. SAUTÉ for 2 minutes, stirring occasionally. Until onion is tender. Stir in the tomatoes, water, clam juice, and sherry. and season with red pepper, salt, and pepper
5. Mix the parsley, shrimp, and fish into the stew. Assemble pressure lid, making sure the pressure release valve is in the SEAL position.
6. Select PRESSURE and set to HIGH. Set time to 5 minutes. Select START/STOP to begin.
7. When pressure cooking is complete, allow pressure to natural release for 10 minutes. After 10 minutes, quick release remaining pressure by turning the pressure release valve to the VENT position. Carefully remove lid when unit has finished releasing pressure.
8. Stir to combine. Top with parsley and serve .

Nutrition Facts

Calories 392, Total Fat 7.2g, Saturated Fat 1.3g, Cholesterol 270mg, Sodium 1152mg, Total Carbohydrate 26.1g, Dietary Fiber 4.3g, Total Sugars 12.1g, Protein 54.5g

Shrimp and Eggplant Gumbo

(Prep Time: 15 min |Cooking Time: 25 min | serve: 2)

Ingredients

- 1 pound medium shrimp - peeled and deveined
- Salt and pepper to taste
- Cayenne pepper to taste
- 1/4 cup coconut oil
- 1 cup chopped eggplant
- ½ tablespoon tomato paste
- 1 tomato, chopped
- ½ cup chopped onion
- 1 teaspoon garlic powder
- 1/2 cup chopped green bell pepper
- 12 cups water
- 1/2 cup chopped green onions

Preparation

1. Select SEAR/SAUTÉ and set to MD:HI. Select START/STOP to begin. Allow to preheat for 5 minutes.
2. Season the shrimp with salt, pepper and cayenne to taste and set aside.
3. After 5 minutes, add oil to the pot. Add the eggplant and sauté for 3 minutes,. Add the tomato paste, tomato, onion, garlic powder and green bell pepper and saute for 15 more minutes.
4. Add the water and season to taste. Add the shrimp Finally, add the green
5. Assemble pressure lid, making sure the pressure release valve is in the SEAL position. Select PRESSURE and set to HIGH. Set time to 4 minutes. Select START/STOP to begin.
6. When pressure cooking is complete, allow pressure to release naturally for 10 minutes. After 10 minutes, quick release any remaining pressure by moving the pressure release valve to the VENT position. Carefully remove lid when unit has finished releasing pressure.

Nutrition Facts

Calories 504, Total Fat 30.3g, Saturated Fat 23.6g, Cholesterol 446mg, Sodium 568mg, Total Carbohydrate 12.3g, Dietary Fiber 3.8g, Total Sugars 6.2g, Protein 50.8g

Crispy Fried Salmon

(Prep Time: 10 min |Cooking Time: 10 min | serve: 2)

Ingredients

- 1 tablespoon butter
- ¼ cup Honey Mustard
- ½ teaspoon kosher salt
- ½ cup panko bread crumbs
- 2 uncooked Salmon fillets

Preparation

1. Place butter, honey mustard, and salt in a bowl and whisk to combine. Add panko bread crumbs to another bowl and stir to combine.
2. Working in small batches, coat fish fillets in mustard mixture. Transfer fillets to bread crumb mixture, tossing well to evenly coat. Set aside.
3. Insert crisper plate in basket and basket in unit. Preheat unit by selecting AIR FRY, setting temperature to 390°F, and setting time to 3 minutes. Select START/STOP to begin preheating.
4. Spray breaded fillets liberally with cooking spray. Once unit is preheated, place fillets on the crisper plate.
5. Select AIR FRY, set temperature to 390°F, and set time to 8 minutes. Select START/STOP to begin cooking.
6. After 4 minutes, remove basket and flip fillets. Reinsert basket to resume cooking.
7. When cooking is complete, serve fish immediately.

Nutrition Facts

Calories 453, Total Fat 18.2g, Saturated Fat 5.5g, Cholesterol 94mg, Sodium 1048mg, Total Carbohydrate 31.4g, Dietary Fiber 1.2g, Total Sugars 7.7g, Protein 38.2g

Jambalaya

(Prep Time: 10 min |Cooking Time: 10 min | serve: 2)

Ingredients

- ½ pound chicken thighs, cut into bite-size pieces
- ¼ cup carrot
- ½ cup diced tomatoes
- ¼ cup chopped green bell pepper
- ½ teaspoon garlic powder
- 1 cup vegetable Broth
- 1 tablespoon Cajun seasoning
- 1 teaspoon dried thyme
- 1 teaspoon dried oregano
- ½ cup uncooked medium shrimp, peeled and deveined
- ½ cup long-grain white rice
- 1 tablespoon chopped fresh mint

Preparation

1. Combine chicken, add rice and shrimp, carrot mix, diced tomatoes, bell pepper, garlic, vegetable Broth, Cajun seasoning, thyme, and oregano in a Ninja foodi. Assemble pressure lid, making sure the pressure release valve is in the SEAL position. Select PRESSURE and set to high (HI). Set time to 25 minutes. Select START/STOP to begin.
2. When pressure cooking is complete, allow pressure to natural release for 10 minutes. After 10 minutes, quick release any remaining pressure by turning the pressure release valve to the VENT position. Carefully remove lid when unit has finished releasing pressure.
3. Let stand, covered, for at least 15 minutes to allow rice to absorb most of the remaining liquid. Garnish with fresh parsley, if desired.

Nutrition Facts

Calories 449, Total Fat 9.9g, Saturated Fat 2.6g, Cholesterol 142mg, Sodium 617mg, Total Carbohydrate 43.2g, Dietary Fiber 2.5g, Total Sugars 3.2g, Protein 44.1g

Mahi Mahi and Coconut Stew

(Prep Time: 15 min |Cooking Time: 20 min | serve: 2)

Ingredients

- 1 tablespoon coconut oil, divided, or as needed
- 1 pounds fresh Mahi mahi, sliced into fillets
- Salt and ground black pepper to taste
- 1 small sweet onion, sliced
- 1 red bell pepper, sliced
- 1 teaspoon garlic powder
- ½ cup diced tomatoes
- ½ cup coconut milk
- 1 Celery chopped

Preparation

1. Rub enough coconut oil onto mahi mahi fillets to coat; season with salt and pepper.
2. Select SEAR/SAUTÉ and set to MD: HI. Select START/STOP to begin. Allow to preheat for 5 minutes.
3. Add coconut oil sauté onion, red bell pepper, and garlic powder until tender, about 2 minutes. Stir diced tomatoes into onion mixture. Arrange MAhi mahi fillets on top of tomato mixture and pour coconut milk over fillets. Sprinkle green onion over MAhi mahi fillets
4. Assemble pressure lid, making sure the pressure release valve is in the SEAL position. Select PRESSURE and set to high (HI). Set time to15 minutes. Select START/STOP to begin.
5. When pressure cooking is complete, allow pressure to natural release for 10 minutes. After 10 minutes, quick release any remaining pressure by turning the pressure release valve to the VENT position. Carefully remove lid when unit has finished releasing pressure.

Nutrition Facts

Calories 446, Total Fat 23.5g, Saturated Fat 19.5g, Cholesterol 171mg, Sodium 231mg, Total Carbohydrate 14.5g, Dietary Fiber 3.9g, Total Sugars 8.3g, Protein 45.3g

Tomato-Rich Fish Stew

(Prep Time: 15 min |Cooking Time: 20 min | serve: 2)

Ingredients

- ½ cup sun-dried tomatoes
- 1 tablespoons coconut oil
- 1 small yellow onion, chopped
- ¼ green bell pepper, chopped
- ¼ cup diced tomatoes
- ¼ teaspoon garlic powder
- 1 tablespoons fresh thyme
- 1 bay leaves
- ¼ cup olives, sliced
- ¼ cup chickpeas, drained and rinsed
- ¼ pound tuna, cut in 2- to 3-inch chunks
- ¼ teaspoons celery seeds, lightly crushed
- 1 pinch Salt and pepper, to taste
- 1tablespoon grated goat cheese

Preparation

1. In a pan, simmer sun-dried tomatoes in 1 1/2 cups water until very soft; discard water.
2. Select SEAR/SAUTÉ and set to MD: HI. Select START/STOP to begin. Allow to preheat for 5 minutes. Sauté onion and green pepper in oil until softened.
3. In a food processor or blender, combine sun-dried tomatoes and water until smooth; add to pot. Add diced tomatoes, garlic powder, thyme, bay leaves and olives.
4. Add beans, fish, celery seeds, salt and pepper. Assemble pressure lid, making sure the pressure release valve is in the SEAL position. Select PRESSURE and set to high (HI). Set time to15 minutes. Select START/STOP to begin.
5. When pressure cooking is complete, allow pressure to natural release for 10 minutes. After 10 minutes, quick release any remaining pressure by turning the pressure release valve to the VENT position. Carefully remove lid when unit has finished releasing pressure.
6. Remove bay leaves. Ladle into bowls; sprinkle with cheese.

Nutrition Facts

Calories 372, Total Fat 20.1g, Saturated Fat 10.8g, Cholesterol 32mg, Sodium 235mg, Total Carbohydrate 24.1g, Dietary Fiber 7g, Total Sugars 6.5g, Protein 25.5g

Shredded Sweet Potato Cod Cakes

(Prep Time: 15 min |Cooking Time: 20 min | serve: 2)

Ingredients

- ½ Sweet potatoes, peeled and shredded
- 1 egg
- Salt and pepper to taste
- ¼ teaspoon Italian seasoning
- ¼ cup cooked flaked salmon
- 1 green onions, chopped
- ¼ tablespoons capers, drained
- ¼ red bell pepper, seeded and chopped
- 3/4 cup dry bread crumbs
- 1 tablespoon oil for frying, or as needed

Preparation

1. Squeeze as much liquid from the sweet potatoes as you can, and place in a large bowl. Beat the eggs with salt, pepper, and Italian seasoning, and mix with the sweet potatoes. Mix in salmon, green onions, capers, red bell pepper and bread crumbs. Form into about 12 patties about 3/4 inch thick.
2. Select AIR FRY, set temperature to 390°F, and set time to 8 minutes. Select START/STOP to begin cooking.
3. After 4 minutes, remove basket and flip fillets. Reinsert basket to resume cooking.
4. When cooking is complete, serve fish immediately

Nutrition Facts

Calories 340, Total Fat 13g, Saturated Fat 2.3g, Cholesterol 96mg, Sodium 375mg, Total Carbohydrate 41.6g, Dietary Fiber 3.8g, Total Sugars 3.8g, Protein 14g

TIME
SEAR/SAUTÉ
BROIL

Chapter 5 Poultry and Meat

Crumbed Chicken Tenderloins

(Prep Time: 15 min |Cooking Time: 10 min | serve: 2)

Ingredients

- 1 egg
- ¼ cup panko bread crumbs
- 1 tablespoons coconut oil
- 4 chicken tenderloins

Preparation

1. Preheat the unit by selecting AIR FRY, setting the temperature to 360°F, and setting the time to 3 minutes. Select START/PAUSE to begin.
2. Whisk egg in a small bowl.
3. Mix bread crumbs and oil together in a second bowl until mixture becomes loose and crumbly.
4. Dip each chicken tenderloin into the bowl of egg; shake off any residual egg. Dip chicken into the crumb mixture, making sure it is evenly and fully covered. Lay chicken tenderloins into the basket of the air fryer .Select AIR FRY, set temperature to 360°F, and set time to 15 minutes. Select START/PAUSE to begin.
5. After 7 minutes, select START/PAUSE to pause cooking. Remove basket from unit and rotate peppers to ensure the bacon crisps on all sides. Reinsert basket and select START/PAUSE to resume cooking.
6. When cooking is complete, remove peppers and allow to cool for 10 minutes and then serve warm.

Nutrition Facts

Calories 309, Total Fat 10.6g, Saturated Fat 1.8g, Cholesterol 131mg, Sodium 754mg, Total Carbohydrate 11.8g, Dietary Fiber 0.6g, Total Sugars 0.9g, Protein 39.2g

Garlic Turkey

(Prep Time: 15 min |Cooking Time: 10 min | serve: 2)

Ingredients

- 2 tablespoons coconut oil
- 2teaspoons garlic powder
- 2 tablespoons bread crumbs
- 1 tablespoon grated goat cheese
- 2 skinless, boneless turkey breast halves

Preparation

1. Preheat the unit by selecting AIR FRY, setting the temperature to 360°F, and setting the time to 3 minutes. Select START/PAUSE to begin.
2. Heat olive oil and garlic in a small saucepan over low heat until warmed, 1 to 2 minutes. Transfer garlic and oil to a shallow bowl.
3. Combine bread crumbs and goat cheese in a separate shallow bowl.
4. Dip turkey breasts in the olive oil-garlic mixture using tongs; transfer to bread crumb mixture and turn to evenly coat. Transfer coated turkey to a shallow baking dish.
5. Select AIR FRY, set temperature to 360°F, and set time to 30 minutes. Select START/PAUSE to begin.
6. After 7 minutes, select START/PAUSE to pause cooking. Remove basket from unit and rotate peppers to ensure the bacon crisps on all sides. Reinsert basket and select START/PAUSE to resume cooking.
7. When cooking is complete, allow to cool for 10 minutes and then serve warm.

Nutrition Facts

Calories 262, Total Fat 17.1g, Saturated Fat 3.6g, Cholesterol 66mg, Sodium 71mg, Total Carbohydrate 1.7g, Dietary Fiber 0.1g,, Total Sugars 0.1g, Protein 25.8g

Braised Red wine Chicken

(Prep Time: 15 min |Cooking Time: 10 min | serve: 2)

Ingredients

- 1 teaspoon dried basil
- 1 teaspoon dried oregano
- 1 teaspoon dried rosemary
- ½ teaspoon dried thyme
- 2 skinless, boneless chicken breast halves
- 1 teaspoon garlic salt
- Ground black pepper to taste
- 2 tablespoons coconut oil
- 1 onion, thinly sliced
- 1 cup diced tomatoes
- ¼ cup red wine vinegar

Preparation

1. Select SEAR/SAUTÉ and set to MD: HI. Select START/STOP to begin. Allow to preheat for 5 minutes.
2. Meanwhile, Season both sides of chicken breasts with garlic salt and pepper.
3. After 5 minutes, add oil to the pot. Cook seasoned chicken breasts until chicken is browned, 3 to 4 minutes per side. Add onion; cook and stir until onion is browned, 3 to 4 minutes.
4. Pour diced tomatoes and red wine vinegar over chicken; season with basil, oregano, rosemary and thyme.
5. Assemble pressure lid, making sure the pressure release valve is in the SEAL position. Select PRESSURE and set to HIGH. Set time to 10 minutes. Select START/STOP to begin.
6. When pressure cooking is complete, allow pressure to release naturally for 10 minutes. After 10 minutes, quick release any remaining pressure by moving the pressure release valve to the VENT position. Carefully remove lid when unit has finished releasing pressure.

Nutrition Facts

Calories 312, Total Fat 18g, Saturated Fat 13.4g, Cholesterol 65mg, Sodium 49mg, Total Carbohydrate 11g, Dietary Fiber 3.1g, Total Sugars 5.2g, Protein 26.8g

Sweet, Sticky and Spicy Chicken

(Prep Time: 10 min |Cooking Time: 15 min | serve: 2)

Ingredients

- ¼ tablespoon maple syrup
- 2 tablespoons honey
- ¼ cup soy sauce
- 1 teaspoon ginger powder
- 1 teaspoon garlic powder
- 2 tablespoons hot sauce
- Salt and pepper to taste
- 2 skinless, boneless Chicken breast halves - cut into 1/2 inch strips
- 1 tablespoon coconut oil

Preparation

1. Select SEAR/SAUTÉ and set to MD: HI. Select START/STOP to begin. Allow to preheat for 5 minutes.
2. Mix together maple syrup, honey, soy sauce, ginger powder, garlic powder and hot sauce in a small bowl.
3. Lightly salt and pepper the Chicken strips.
4. Assemble pressure lid, making sure the pressure release valve is in the SEAL position. Select PRESSURE and set to HIGH. Set time to 05 minutes. Select START/STOP to begin.
5. When pressure cooking is complete, allow pressure to release naturally for 10 minutes. After 10 minutes, quick release any remaining pressure by moving the pressure release valve to the VENT position. Carefully remove lid when unit has finished releasing pressure.

Nutrition Facts

Calories 293, Total Fat 10.9g, Saturated Fat 7.4g, Cholesterol 65mg, Sodium 2219mg, Total Carbohydrate 22.9g, Dietary Fiber 0.5g, Total Sugars 19.8g, Protein 27.4g

Coconut Turkey

(Prep Time: 10 min |Cooking Time: 25 min | serve: 2)

Ingredients

- ½ cup boneless skinless turkey breasts, cut into 1/2-inch chunks
- ¼ teaspoon salt and pepper, or to taste
- ½ tablespoon coconut oil
- 1 tablespoon curry powder
- ½ onion, thinly sliced
- ½ teaspoon garlic powder
- 1 cup coconut milk
- 1cup diced tomatoes
- ½ cup tomato sauce
- 1 tablespoon honey

Preparation

1. Select SEAR/SAUTÉ and set to MD: HI. Select START/STOP to begin. Allow to preheat for 5 minutes.
2. Meanwhile, Season turkey pieces with salt and pepper.
3. After 5 minutes, add coconut oil and curry powder Stir in onions and garlic, and cook 1 minute more. Add turkey, tossing lightly to coat with curry oil.
4. Pour coconut milk, tomatoes, tomato sauce, and honey into the pan, and stir to combine.
5. Assemble pressure lid, making sure the pressure release valve is in the SEAL position. Select PRESSURE and set to HIGH. Set time to 25 minutes. Select START/STOP to begin.
6. When pressure cooking is complete, allow pressure to release naturally for 10 minutes. After 10 minutes, quick release any remaining pressure by moving the pressure release valve to the VENT position. Carefully remove lid when unit has finished releasing pressure.

Nutrition Facts

Calories 432, Total Fat 36.4g, Saturated Fat 31.4g, Cholesterol 5mg, Sodium 456mg, Total Carbohydrate 27.5g, Dietary Fiber 6.4g, Total Sugars 19.4g, Protein 7g

Chicken and Wild Rice Soup

(Prep Time: 20 min |Cooking Time: 15 min | serve: 2)

Ingredients

- 2 cups chicken broth
- 1 cup water
- 1 cup boneless chicken breast halves, shredded
- ½ cup quick cooking long grain and wild rice
- ½ teaspoon salt
- ½ teaspoon ground black pepper
- ¾ cup coconut flour
- 1 tablespoon coconut oil
- 1cup coconut cream

Preparation

1. Combine broth, water and chicken, rice in ninja foodi.
2. Assemble pressure lid, making sure the pressure release valve is in the SEAL position. Select PRESSURE and set to HIGH. Set time to 2 minutes. Select START/STOP to begin.
3. When pressure cooking is complete, allow pressure to naturally release for 10 minutes. After 10 minutes, quick release remaining pressure by moving the pressure release valve to the VENT position. Carefully remove lid when unit has finished releasing pressure.
4. In a small bowl, combine salt, pepper and flour. In a medium saucepan over medium heat, melt butter. Stir in contents of seasoning packet until mixture is bubbly.
5. Select SEAR/SAUTÉ and set to HIGH. Add mixer simmer for 5 minutes to heat through. Season with salt and pepper to taste. Add additional water as needed to achieve desired consistency.
6. When cooking is complete, serve immediately.

Nutrition Facts

Calories 323, Total Fat 20.1g, Saturated Fat 16.5g, Cholesterol 27mg, Sodium 712mg, Total Carbohydrate 20.4g, Dietary Fiber 3.6g, Total Sugars 3g, Protein 17.3g

Artichoke Turkey

(Prep Time: 10 min |Cooking Time: 20 min | serve: 2)

Ingredients

- ½ cup artichoke hearts, drained and chopped
- ¼ cup grated Mozzarella cheese
- ¼ cup Greek Yogurt
- 1 pinch garlic pepper
- 2 skinless, boneless turkey breast halves

Preparation

1. In a medium bowl, mix together the artichoke hearts, mozzarella cheese, Greek Yogurt, and garlic pepper. Place turkey in a greased baking dish, and cover evenly with artichoke mixture.
2. Assemble pressure lid, making sure the pressure release valve is in the SEAL position. Select PRESSURE and set to high (HI). Set time to 22 minutes. Select START/STOP to begin.
3. When pressure cooking is complete, allow pressure to natural release for 5 minutes. After 5 minutes, quick release the pressure by moving the pressure release valve to the VENT position. Carefully remove lid when unit has finished releasing pressure.
4. Close crisping lid. Select AIR CRISP, set temperature to 400°F, and set time to 8 minutes. Select START/STOP to begin. Cook until desired level of crispness is reached, adding up to 10 additional minutes.

Nutrition Facts

Calories 188, Total Fat 5.2g, Saturated Fat 2.3g, Cholesterol 68mg, Sodium 125mg, Total Carbohydrate 5.4g, Dietary Fiber 2.2g, Total Sugars 1.4g, Protein 29.8g

Turkey Wings

(Prep Time: 10 min |Cooking Time: 25 min | serve: 2)

Ingredients

- 2 pounds turkey wings, rinsed, patted dry
- 2 tablespoons coconut oil
- ¼ cup hot sauce

Preparation

1. In a large mixing bowl, toss turkey wings with coconut oil until evenly coated.
2. Insert crisper basket in unit. Select AIR CRISP, set temperature to 390°F, and set time to 26 minutes. Select START/STOP to begin preheating.
3. When the unit beeps to signify it has preheated, place wings in basket, spreading out evenly. Close hood and cook for 12 minutes.
4. After 12 minutes, stir wings with rubber-tipped tongs. Close hood and cook for 12 more minutes.
5. After 12 minutes, remove wings from basket. For additional crispiness, cook wings up to an additional 2 minutes.
6. When cooking is complete, transfer wings to a large mixing bowl, pour hot sauce over them, and use rubber-tipped tongs to mix wings with sauce. Serve immediately.

Nutrition Facts

Calories 331, Total Fat 22g, Saturated Fat 14.7g, Cholesterol 102mg, Sodium 847mg, Total Carbohydrate 0.5g, Dietary Fiber 0.1g, Total Sugars 0.4g, Protein 32g

Peanut Butter Chicken

(Prep Time: 10 min |Cooking Time: 30 min | serve: 2)

Ingredients

- 1 tablespoon coconut oil
- 4 skinless boneless chicken thighs, cut into chunks
- ½ teaspoon garlic powder
- 1 red chillies, finely sliced
- ½ teaspoon ginger powder
- 1 teaspoon Garam masala
- ½ teaspoon peanut butter
- 1 cup soy milk
- ½ cup chopped tomatoes
- 1 small bunch parsley
- Roasted peanuts, to serve

Preparation

1. Select SEAR/SAUTÉ and set to MD: HI. Select START/STOP to begin. Allow to preheat for 5 minutes.
2. After 5 minutes, add coconut oil and Brown the chicken in batches, setting aside once golden. Fry the garlic, chilli and ginger in the other 1 tablespoon oil for 1 min. Add the Garam masala and fry for 1 min more.
3. Stir in the peanut butter, soy milk and tomatoes, and bring to a simmer. Return the chicken to the pan and add the chopped parsley
4. Assemble pressure lid, making sure the pressure release valve is in the SEAL position. Select PRESSURE and set to HIGH. Set time to 25 minutes. Select START/STOP to begin.
5. When pressure cooking is complete, allow pressure to release naturally for 10 minutes. After 10 minutes, quick release any remaining pressure by moving the pressure release valve to the VENT position. Carefully remove lid when unit has finished releasing pressure

Nutrition Facts

Calories 390, Total Fat 26.8g, Saturated Fat 10.3g, Cholesterol 90mg, Sodium 153mg, Total Carbohydrate 13.7g, Dietary Fiber 2.9g, Total Sugars 7g, Protein 27.9g

Turkey Curry

(Prep Time: 10 min |Cooking Time: 30 min | serve: 2)

Ingredients

- 1 cup boneless diced turkey
- ½ tablespoon plain yoghurt
- 2 tablespoon Garam masala
- ½ tablespoon coconut oil
- 1 green chillies
- ½ tablespoon ginger and garlic paste
- ½ teaspoon turmeric
- ½ cup tomatoes
- 1 onions, chopped
- Salt, to taste
- Basil, to garnish

Preparation

1. Marinate the turkey with the yoghurt, Garam masala, and ½ tablespoon of ginger and garlic paste. Refrigerate overnight. Remove and bring to room temperature before cooking.
2. Select SEAR/SAUTÉ and set to MD. Select START/STOP to begin. Allow to preheat for 5 minutes.
3. Add the coconut oil to the pot. When the coconut oil begins to sizzle, add the onions and chillies. Stir until the onions are soft.
4. Add the turkey and fry until the turkey pieces start to become opaque.
5. Add the tomatoes, remaining 1 tablespoons of garam masala, the turmeric, salt, and remaining ginger garlic paste and stir.
6. Add the hot water and stir until thoroughly mixed.
7. Assemble the pressure lid, making sure the pressure release valve is in the SEAL position. Select PRESSURE and set to HIGH. Set time to 10 minutes and select START/STOP to begin.
8. When the pressure cooking is complete, quick release the pressure by moving the pressure release valve to the VENT position. Carefully remove the lid when the unit has finished releasing pressure.
9. Serve with coriander to garnish.

Nutrition Facts

Calories 172, Total Fat 9.9g, Saturated Fat 5.5g, Cholesterol 38mg, Sodium 578mg, Total Carbohydrate 10.5g, Dietary Fiber 1.9g, Total Sugars 4g, Protein 7.8g

Chapter 6 Beef Lamb and Pork

Fragrant Beef & Eggplant Stew

(Prep Time: 10 min |Cooking Time: 20 min | serve: 2)

Ingredients

- ½ tablespoon coconut oil
- 1small onion, diced
- 1 teaspoon garlic powder
- 1 small red chilli, finely chopped
- 1 Eggplant, diced
- ½ teaspoon ground cumin
- ½ teaspoon ground coriander
- 1 teaspoon chilli powder
- 2 tomatoes, diced
- ½ cup beef, cut into pieces
- 1 cup beef stock

Preparation

1. Turn on your Foodi and press the sauté button. Set to the Med heat setting and allow to heat for 5 minutes
2. Add the coconut oil along with the onion, garlic and chilli and sauté for 5 minutes, stirring occasionally until the onion begins to brown
3. Add the eggplant and sauté for a further 3 minutes before adding the cumin, coriander and chilli powder. Stir in the spices so everything is well combined
4. Add the tomatoes to the pot, stir, then add the beef and beef stock. Stir one more time to ensure everything is combined
5. Click the 'Stop' button, and assemble the pressure lid, making sure the valve sealed
6. Select pressure and set to low. Set time to 20 minutes, then click START
7. When cooking is complete, carefully turn the valve to the vent position
8. Once all the pressure has been released, carefully remove the lid, serve and enjoy!\

Nutrition Facts

Calories 185, Total Fat 5.9g, Saturated Fat 3.5g, Cholesterol 19mg, Sodium 27mg, Total Carbohydrate 25.3g, Dietary Fiber 11.5g, Total Sugars 11.9g, Protein 11.2g

Panko Lamb Bites

(Prep Time: 20 min |Cooking Time: 15 min | serve: 2)

Ingredients

- 1 cup boneless lamb breast , cut into pieces
- 1 tablespoon coconut flour
- ½ teaspoon sriracha
- Juice from 1/2 lime
- ½ teaspoon soy sauce
- Pinch of salt
- ¼ cup panko bread crumbs
- 1 teaspoon fresh basil

Preparation

1. Start by making the batter. Combine coconut flour, sriracha, salt, lime juice and soy sauce
2. Place panko bread crumbs into a bowl, and then dip each beef floret into the batter before coating thoroughly with breadcrumbs
3. Add to your Ninja Foodi, and cook on air crisp setting at 200C for 10 minutes
4. Serve with sauce and chopped basil

Nutrition Facts

Calories 296, Total Fat 13.7g, Saturated Fat 6.6g, Cholesterol 40mg, Sodium 298mg, Total Carbohydrate 15.9g, Dietary Fiber 3.2g, Total Sugars 1.7g, Protein 9.5g

Slow Cooked Sweet Potato Pork Chilli

(Prep Time: 20 min |Cooking Time: 5 hr.| serve: 2)

Ingredients

- ½ medium sweet potato, peeled and cut into cubes
- ½ cup chickpeas, drained and rinsed
- ½ cup pork , cut into pieces
- ½ cup chopped tomatoes
- 1 small red onion, chopped
- 1 teaspoon garlic powder
- 1 tablespoon chilli powder
- 1 teaspoon cumin
- 1/8 teaspoon ground nutmeg
- ½ teaspoon salt
- ¼ teaspoon black pepper

Preparation

1. In the Ninja Foodi, combine the red onion, red pepper, garlic, chilli powder, cumin, nutmeg, salt and black pepper. Add the chopped tomatoes (with the liquid), sweet potato, chickpeas , pork and 1 cup water
2. Place the pressure lid on to the Foodi, select slow cook and put on either low for 8 hours, or on high for 5 hours
3. Serve the chilli topped with guacamole, chopped spring onion, radishes and tortilla chips.

Nutrition Facts

Calories 294, Total Fat 5.2g, Saturated Fat 0.6g, Cholesterol 16mg, Sodium 622mg, Total Carbohydrate 46.3g, Dietary Fiber 13.4g, Total Sugars 10.2g, Protein 17.8g

Lamb Fingers

(Prep Time: 20 min |Cooking Time: 10 min.| serve: 2)

Ingredients

- ½ cup crushed cornflakes
- 1 tablespoon fresh coriander, stems removed and chopped
- ¼ teaspoon garlic minced
- Sea salt and pepper (to taste)
- ¼ cup coconut flour
- 1eggs whisked
- 8 mini lamb fillers

Preparation

1. Cover each lamb fillet in coconut flour, then dip in the egg mixture and coat in cornflakes crushed . Follow until all of the lamb fillets are coated
2. Place the cook and crisp basket into the Foodi, close the lid and press the BAKE/ROAST setting at 200°C. Set for 5 minutes to preheat. Spray fillets with oil and place half in the basket. Set timer to 10 minutes. Cook in batches until done(75°C) and flip halfway through
3. Spray fillets with oil and place half of them in the basket. Set the timer to 10 minutes. Cook in batches until done, flipping halfway through.

Nutrition Facts

Calories 310, Total Fat 9.6g, Saturated Fat 4g, Cholesterol 158mg, Sodium 286mg, Total Carbohydrate 24.3g, Dietary Fiber 3.8g, Total Sugars 1.7g, Protein 29.7g

Pork Lettuce Wraps

(Prep Time: 60 min |Cooking Time: 10 min.| serve: 2)

Ingredients

- ¼ cup basmati rice
- ½ cup water
- ½ boneless pork ribs, sliced thinly to 5mm
- ¼ large zucchini, sliced into half moons
- 2 heads baby cos lettuce leaves, cleaned and patted dry
- 1 leek, sliced thinly
- Soy sauce for serving

For the marinade

- 1 tablespoon low sodium soy sauce
- 1 tablespoon honey
- ½ tablespoon olive oil
- ½ teaspoon chilli flakes
- 1 teaspoon garlic powder
- 1 teaspoon ginger powder

Preparation

1. Place the pork and all the marinade Ingredients into a plastic bag and seal shut, refrigerate for 1-2 hours at least
2. Place the rice and water into the Foodi bowl. Assemble the pressure lid, making sure the pressure release valve is in the SEAL position
3. Select PRESSURE and set to HIGH. Set time to 2 minutes. Press START/STOP to begin. Allow the pressure to naturally release for 10 minutes. Once finished, press the quick release valve to ensure all pressure has been removed. Take out the rice, place it in a bowl and cover. Wash the Foodi bowl and return to machine.
4. Press SEAR/SAUTE and set to Med/High. Allow to warm up for 5 minutes
5. Place the pork in to the Foodi, stirring occasionally until cooked through
6. To serve assemble few tablespoons of rice on each leaf, with pork, zucchini and, and sprinkle with leek.

Nutrition Facts

Calories 242, Total Fat 4.7g, Saturated Fat 0.8g, Cholesterol 16mg, Sodium 780mg, Total Carbohydrate 39.8g, Dietary Fiber 2.9g, Total Sugars 11.8g, Protein 10.7g

Beef Grains, Greens Bowl

(Prep Time: 45 min |Cooking Time: 10 min.| serve: 2)

Ingredients

- 1 tablespoon soy sauce, divided
- 1teaspoon honey
- 2 tablespoons avocado oil, divided
- 1 teaspoon garlic powder
- ½ cup beef cut into 1.5cm cubes
- ¼ cup wheat berries, rinsed
- ¼ cup wild rice, rinsed
- 1 cup vegetable stock or water
- ½ spinach, sliced

Preparation

1. In a large bowl, stir together 1 tablespoons soy sauce, honey avocado oil, and garlic powder. Add the beef and coat in the marinade, leave for at least 15 minutes.
2. Place the wheat berries, wild rice, stock or water, spinach, remaining soy sauce, and avocado oil to the pot. Assemble the pressure lid, making sure the pressure release valve is in the SEAL position.
3. Select PRESSURE and set to HIGH. Set time to 10 minutes. Select START/STOP to begin.
4. When the pressure cooking is complete, quick release the pressure by moving the pressure release valve to the VENT position. Carefully remove the lid when the unit has finished releasing pressure.
5. Place the Reversible Rack inside the pot over the rice, making sure rack is in the higher position. Cover rack with aluminium foil, then place beef on the rack.
6. Close the crisping lid. Select AIR CRISP, set temperature to 160°C, and set time to 15 minutes. Select START/STOP to begin. Halfway through cooking, flip the tofu.
7. When the cooking is complete, add the tofu to the grains and greens and serve with your favourite toppings.

Nutrition Facts

Calories 200, Total Fat 4.8g, Saturated Fat 2g, Cholesterol 19mg, Sodium 897mg, Total Carbohydrate 30.1g, Dietary Fiber 4.1g, Total Sugars 5.3g, Protein 13.8g

Garlic Lamb with Risotto

(Prep Time: 45 min |Cooking Time: 10 min.| serve: 2)

Ingredients

- 1 tablespoon coconut oil, divided
- 1 small onion
- 2 teaspoons garlic powder
- ½ cup vegetable stock
- ¼ cup Arborio rice
- ½ cup lamb, cut into pieces
- ¼ teaspoon ground black pepper
- 1 tablespoon butter
- Juice of 1 lemon
- ½ cup broccoli, cut into 2.5cm pieces
- ¼ cup grated goat cheese, plus more for serving

Preparation

1. Select SEAR/SAUTÉ and set to MD:HI. Select START/STOP to begin. Allow to preheat for 5 minutes.
2. Add ½ tablespoon coconut oil to the pot and add the onion. Sauté until softened, about 5 minutes. Add half the garlic powder and cook until fragrant, about 1 minute. Season with 2 teaspoons salt.
3. Add the stock and rice to the pot. Assemble the pressure lid, making sure the pressure release valve is in the SEAL position. Select PRESSURE and set to HIGH. Set time to 7 minutes. Select START/STOP to begin.
4. While the rice is cooking, toss the lamb in the remaining oil, garlic powder, salt, black pepper, and crushed red pepper in a mixing bowl.
5. When the pressure cooking is complete, allow pressure to natural release for 10 minutes. After 10 minutes, quick release remaining pressure by moving the pressure release valve to the VENT position. Carefully remove lid when the unit has finished releasing pressure.
6. Stir the butter, lemon juice, and broccoli into the rice until evenly incorporated.
7. Place the Reversible Rack inside the pot over risotto, making sure rack is in the higher position. Place lamb on the rack.
8. Close the crisping lid. Select GRILL and set time to 8 minutes. Select START/STOP to begin.
9. When the cooking is complete, remove the rack from the pot. Stir parmesan into the risotto. Top with lamb and parmesan and serve immediately.

Nutrition Facts

Calories 284, Total Fat 15.7g, Saturated Fat 11g, Cholesterol 38mg, Sodium 93mg, Total Carbohydrate 26.2g, Dietary Fiber 2.5g, Total Sugars 2.8g, Protein 10.3g

Pork Curry

(Prep Time: 45 min |Cooking Time: 10 min.| serve: 2)

Ingredients

- 1 boneless diced pork chop
- ½ tablespoon plain yoghurt
- 2 tablespoon Garam masala
- ½ tablespoon coconut oil
- 1 green chillies
- ½ tablespoon ginger and garlic paste
- ½ teaspoon turmeric
- ½ cup tomatoes
- 1 onions, chopped
- 1 cup hot water
- Salt, to taste

Preparation

1. Marinate the pork with the yoghurt, 1 tablespoons of Garam masala, and ½ tablespoon of ginger and garlic paste. Refrigerate overnight. Remove and bring to room temperature before cooking.
2. Select SEAR/SAUTÉ and set to MD. Select START/STOP to begin. Allow to preheat for 5 minutes.
3. Add the coconut oil to the pot. When the coconut oil begins to sizzle, add the onions and chillies. Stir until the onions are soft.
4. Add the pork and fry until the pork pieces start to become opaque.
5. Add the tinned tomatoes, remaining 1 tablespoons of Garam masala, the turmeric, salt, and remaining ginger garlic paste and stir.
6. Add the hot water and stir until thoroughly mixed.
7. Assemble the pressure lid, making sure the pressure release valve is in the SEAL position. Select PRESSURE and set to HIGH. Set time to 10 minutes and select START/STOP to begin.
8. When the pressure cooking is complete, quick release the pressure by moving the pressure release valve to the VENT position. Carefully remove the lid when the unit has finished releasing pressure.
9. Serve.

Nutrition Facts

Calories 168, Total Fat 6.5g, Saturated Fat 3.9g, Cholesterol 39mg, Sodium 170mg, Total Carbohydrate 10.9g, Dietary Fiber 1.8g, Total Sugars 4g, Protein 15.9g

Garlic Beef Quinoa

(Prep Time: 25 min |Cooking Time: 10 min.| serve: 2)

Ingredients

- 1 tablespoon coconut oil, divided
- 1 small onion, peeled, finely diced
- 2 teaspoon garlic powder
- 1 teaspoon salt, divided
- 2 cups vegetable stock
- ½ cup quinoa
- ½ cup beef cut into pieces
- ½ teaspoon ground black pepper
- ¼ teaspoon crushed red pepper (optional)
- 1 tablespoon butter
- Juice of 1 lime
- 1 bunch asparagus, cut in 1-inch pieces
- ½ cup grated mozzarella cheese

Preparation

1. Select SEAR/SAUTÉ and set to MD:HI. Select START/STOP to begin. Allow to preheat for 5 minutes.
2. Add ½ tablespoon coconut oil to pot and add onion. Sauté until softened, about 5 minutes. Add half the garlic powder and cook until fragrant, about 1 minute. Season with 2 teaspoons salt.
3. Add stock and quinoa to pot. Assemble pressure lid, making sure the pressure release valve is in the SEAL position. Select PRESSURE and set to HIGH. Set time to 7 minutes. Select START/STOP to begin.
4. While rice is cooking, toss beef in the remaining oil, garlic, salt, garlic powder, black pepper, and crushed red pepper in a mixing bowl.
5. When pressure cooking is complete, allow pressure to natural release for 10 minutes. After 10 minutes, quick release remaining pressure by moving the pressure release valve to the VENT position. Carefully remove lid when unit has finished releasing pressure.
6. Stir butter, lemon juice, and asparagus into the quinoa until evenly incorporated.
7. Place Reversible Rack inside pot over risotto, making sure rack is in the higher position. Place beef on rack.
8. Close crisping lid. Select GRILL and set time to 8 minutes. Select START/STOP to begin.
9. When cooking is complete, remove rack from pot. Stir mozzarella into the quinoa. Top with beef and mozzarella and serve immediately.

Nutrition Facts

Calories 393,Total Fat 15.8g,Saturated Fat 10.9g,Cholesterol 38mg, Sodium 1331mg, Total Carbohydrate 49.6g, Dietary Fiber 4.3g, Total Sugars 4g, Protein 14.4g

Lamb, Cauliflower and Spicy Rice

(Prep Time: 25 min |Cooking Time: 10 min.| serve: 2)

Ingredients

- ½ cup grain white rice
- 1 cup chicken stock
- ½ tablespoon soy sauce
- ½ carrots,
- 1 small onions
- ¼ teaspoon garlic powder
- ¼ teaspoon chilli flakes
- Salt and pepper to taste
- 1 cup lamb, cut into pieces
- ½ head cauliflower, trimmed and cut into small florets
- 1 tablespoon olive oil

Preparation

1. Select SEAR/SAUTÉ and set to HI. Select START/STOP to begin. Allow to preheat for 5 minutes.
2. After 5 minutes, add ½ tablespoon oil and the onion. Cook, stirring occasionally, for 3 minutes, until onions are fragrant. Add the white rice, 2 teaspoons salt, and. Cook, stirring frequently, until the rice is coated with oil and very shiny. Add the chicken stock and stir to incorporate.
3. Place lamb breasts on the Reversible Rack, making sure rack is in the higher position. Place the rack inside the pot over rice mixture.
4. Assemble the pressure lid, making sure the pressure release valve is in the SEAL position.
5. Select PRESSURE and set to HIGH. Set time to 22 minutes. Select START/STOP to begin.
6. While the lamb and rice are cooking, toss the cauliflower in a bowl with the remaining oil, salt, and pepper.
7. When the pressure cooking is complete, allow pressure to naturally release for 10 minutes. After 10 minutes, quick release any remaining pressure by moving the pressure release valve to the VENT position. Carefully remove the lid when the unit has finished releasing pressure.

8. Lift the Reversible Rack out of the pot. Stir the parsley into rice, then add the cauliflower directly on top of the rice.
9. Brush the lamb breasts on all sides with honey mustard sauce, then return the Reversible Rack to the pot over the rice and cauliflower.
10. Close the crisping lid. Select GRILL and set time to 10 minutes. Select START/STOP to begin.
11. When the cooking is finished, check that lamb is cooked through. Serve the lamb with cauliflower and rice.

Nutrition Facts

Calories 230, Total Fat 10.6g, Saturated Fat 2.2g, Cholesterol 38mg, Sodium 672mg, Total Carbohydrate 19.1g, Dietary Fiber 3g, Total Sugars 4.4g, Protein 15.4g

Chapter 7 Snacks and Appetizers

Spring Rolls

(Prep Time: 20 min |Cooking Time: 08 min | serve: 2)

Ingredients

- ¼ cup grounded beef
- ½ small onion
- 1 tablespoon salt
- 1 teaspoon ground black pepper
- 2 spring roll wrappers
- 1 egg, lightly beaten
- 1 slices goat cheese, cut in quarters
- Cooking spray

Preparation

1. Place grounded beef, pepper & onion, salt, and pepper in a skillet. Sauté on medium-high heat for 10 minutes, stirring occasionally. Set aside and let cool.
2. Lay out the spring roll wrappers in diamond positions. Brush borders with beaten egg. Place a piece of cheese slightly off centre on a wrapper. Add about 2 tablespoons steak mixture in centre. Fold the left and right edges toward the centre, while simultaneously rolling the wrapper from back to front. Repeat with remaining wrappers.
3. Select AIR FRY, set temperature to 375°F, and set time to 8 minutes. Press START/PAUSE
4. To begin preheating.
5. Meanwhile, liberally spray the air fry basket with cooking spray. Arrange rolls in the basket, making sure to not overcrowd them.
6. When unit has preheated, slide basket into the upper rails of the oven.
7. When cooking is complete, allow to cool before serving

Nutrition Facts

Calories 214, Total Fat 8.8g, Saturated Fat 4.7g, Cholesterol 109mg, Sodium 3761mg, Total Carbohydrate 19.7g, Dietary Fiber 0.9g, Total Sugars 0.5g, Protein 13.4g

Serrano Pepper

(Prep Time: 15 min |Cooking Time:15 min | serve: 2)

Ingredients

- 1 tablespoon Greek yogurt
- 1 tablespoon shredded goat cheese
- 1 teaspoon salt
- 2 Serrano peppers, cut in half lengthwise, stems left on, seeds and membranes removed
- 1strips uncooked bacon

Preparation

1. In a small mixing bowl, mix together the Greek yogurt, goat, and salt.
2. Using a small teaspoon or coffee spoon, fill each Serrano half with the cheese mixture, making sure not to overfill.
3. Place 2 pepper halves together, then wrap each pepper with ½ piece of bacon. Repeat with remaining peppers.
4. Insert crisper plate in basket and basket in unit. Then preheat the unit by selecting AIR FRY, setting the temperature to 360°F, and setting the time to 3 minutes. Select START/PAUSE to begin.
5. After 3 minutes, place peppers on crisper plate; reinsert basket. Select AIR FRY, set temperature to 360°F, and set time to 15 minutes. Select START/PAUSE to begin.
6. After 7 minutes, select START/PAUSE to pause cooking. Remove basket from unit and rotate peppers to ensure the bacon crisps on all sides. Reinsert basket and select START/PAUSE to resume cooking.
7. When cooking is complete, remove peppers and allow to cool for 10 minutes and then serve warm.

Nutrition Facts

Calories 145, Total Fat 7.3g, Saturated Fat 3.7g, Cholesterol 19mg, Sodium 1428mg, Total Carbohydrate 4.7g, Dietary Fiber 0.2g, Total Sugars 4.3g, Protein 14.8g

Guacamole

(Prep Time: 15 min |Cooking Time:15 min | serve: 2)

Ingredients

- 1 tomato
- 1 Serrano pepper top cut off, seeded and chunked
- ¼ cup basil
- ¼ cup lime juice
- ¼ teaspoon ground black pepper
- ½ teaspoon salt
- 1 ripe avocado peeled, pitted and quartered

Preparation

1. Place all Ingredients, in the order that they are listed, into a Ninja chopping bowl.
2. Pulse 5 to 7 times.
3. For creamy guacamole process until completely smooth.

Nutrition Facts

Calories 214, Total Fat 19.7g, Saturated Fat 4.1g, Cholesterol 0mg, Sodium 590mg, Total Carbohydrate 10.8g, Dietary Fiber 7.4g, Total Sugars 1.5g, Protein 2.4g

Crackers

(Prep Time: 10 min |Cooking Time:15 min | serve: 2)

Ingredients

- ¼ cup coconut flour
- ¼ cup almond flour
- ¼ teaspoon salt
- ¼ teaspoon ground black pepper
- ¼ tablespoon olive oil
- ¼ cup water
- ¼ teaspoon fresh thyme

Preparation

1. Preheat oven to 400°F.
2. Place all Ingredients, except water, into the Nutri Bow. PULSE until Ingredients are combined and butter forms pea-sized pieces.
3. Turn the dough out onto a large piece of plastic wrap. Press it into a 1-inch thick disk. Wrap tightly in plastic wrap and refrigerate for 1 hour.
4. Place dough onto a lightly floured surface and roll into a rectangle, about 1/8-inch thick. Place the rolled dough onto an ungreased baking sheet. Prick dough with a fork and cut in desired cracker shapes.
5. Bake 14 minutes, or until light golden brown. Let cool completely.

Nutrition Facts

Calories 104, Total Fat 9g, Saturated Fat 1g, Cholesterol 0mg, Sodium 296mg, Total Carbohydrate 4.3g, Dietary Fiber 2.3g, Total Sugars 0.6g, Protein 3.3g

Apple Basil Flatbread

(Prep Time: 10 min |Cooking Time: 15 min | serve: 2)

Ingredients

- ¼ cup warm water
- ½ tablespoon active dry yeast
- ¼ teaspoon salt
- ¼ tablespoon maple syrup
- 1 tablespoon coconut oil
- ¼ cup coconut flour
- 1/8 cup almond flour
- Cornmeal, for dusting
- 1 small apple, thinly sliced
- ½ teaspoon fresh basil, stems removed, minced
- ½ tablespoon crumbled mozzarella cheese

Preparation

1. Preheat oven to 450°F.
2. Position the Dough Blade Assembly in the Nutri Bowl™, then add water, yeast, salt, and maple syrup; PULSE to combine.
3. Add coconut oil and coconut and almond flours, and select Auto-iQ BOOST YES FUSION DOUGH until a loose ball forms. Transfer dough to a lightly oiled bowl and cover. Let rise for 1 hour.
4. Sprinkle a 10 x 15-inch baking sheet with cornmeal and roll out or press the dough into a thin round. Lay apple slices on top and sprinkle evenly with shredded cheese.
5. Bake 10 to 15 minutes, or until cheese has melted and crust is golden brown. Garnish with fresh basil.

Nutrition Facts

Calories 210, Total Fat 7.2g, Saturated Fat 3.7g, Cholesterol 2mg, Sodium 183mg, Total Carbohydrate 33.9g, Dietary Fiber 4.6g, Total Sugars 6.9g, Protein 5.1g

Stuffed Mushrooms

(Prep Time: 10 min |Cooking Time: 20 min | serve: 2)

Ingredients

- ¼ cup almond, shelled
- ¼ red bell pepper
- ½ green onion, cut in half, seeded
- 1 teaspoon garlic powder
- ¼ cup basil leaves
- 2 oz. low-fat cream cheese
- 1 tablespoon lime juice
- ½ teaspoon lime zest
- ½ teaspoon honey
- ¼ teaspoon. salt
- ¼ cup bread crumbs
- 4 small stuffing mushrooms, cleaned and de-stemmed

Preparation

1. Place the almond in the Nutri Ninja Cup. Press the Single Serve button and pulse until finely chopped. Remove the blades from the cup after blending and set aside.
2. Place the bell pepper, green onion, garlic powder and basil in the Nutri Ninja® Cup. Press the Single Serve button and pulse briefly to chop.
3. Add cream cheese, lime juice and zest, sugar and salt and pulse until smooth.
4. Remove the blades from the cup after blending and hand stir in bread crumbs.
5. Preheat oven to 425 °F. Spoon mixture into mushrooms and arrange in a baking dish. Sprinkle almond over mushrooms and bake for 20 minutes until mushrooms are softened and cheese is puffed and browned on top. Cool slightly before serving.

Nutrition Facts

Calories 124, Total Fat 8.4g, Saturated Fat 3.4g, Cholesterol 16mg, Sodium 93mg, Total Carbohydrate 9.8g, Dietary Fiber 1.5g, Total Sugars 2.4g, Protein 3.9g

Spinach Chips

(Prep Time: 10 min |Cooking Time: 30 min | serve: 2)

Ingredients

- 1 large bunch of Spinach, stems removed, rinsed and ripped into pieces
- 1 teaspoon garlic powder

Preparation

1. Preheat oven to 300 degrees. Place spinach in a bowl and set aside.
2. Add garlic powder to the spinach and toss to coat.
3. Spread the spinach out on a large baking sheet and cook for 30-40 minutes, tossing every 15 minutes or so. Enjoy!

Nutrition Facts

Calories 44, Total Fat 0.7g, Saturated Fat 0.1g, Cholesterol 0mg, Sodium 135mg, Total Carbohydrate 7.2g, Dietary Fiber 3.9g, Total Sugars 1.1g, Protein 5.1g

Spiced Nuts

(Prep Time: 02 min |Cooking Time: 05 min | serve: 2)

Ingredients

- 1 lemon,
- 1 cup mixed nuts,
- 2 tablespoons olive oil,
- 2 tablespoons honey,
- ½ teaspoon paprika,
- ¼ teaspoon ground cumin,
- 1 teaspoon nutmeg,
- 1 tablespoon water

Preparation

1. Grate zest from lemon. Line rimmed baking sheet with parchment paper.
2. Place nuts, olive oil, honey, paprika, cumin, nutmeg and water into Ninja Cooking System pot and set to STOVETOP MED. Cook uncovered 5 minutes or until honey mixture coats the nuts, stirring constantly.
3. Spread nut mixture on baking sheet. Sprinkle with lemon zest. Let stand 10 minutes or until honey mixture is hardened.

Nutrition Facts

Calories 322, Total Fat 27.5g, Saturated Fat 4.4g, Cholesterol 0mg, Sodium 111mg, Total Carbohydrate 18.5g, Dietary Fiber 2.6g, Total Sugars 10.8g, Protein 5.9g

Potato and Beetroots Latkes

(Prep Time: 15 min |Cooking Time: 15 min | serve: 2)

Ingredients

- ½ pound potatoes, peeled and cut into 1" pieces,
- ¼ pound Beetroots, peeled and cut into 1" pieces,
- ½ small onion, cut in quarters,
- 1 teaspoon garlic powder,
- ¼ cup coconut flour,
- 1 eggs, lightly beaten,
- ¼ teaspoon salt,
- 1/8 teaspoon pepper,
- 1 tablespoon coconut oil

Preparation

1. Place the Top Blades in the Ninja Ultima Pitcher and add potato and beetroots. PULSE 3–5 times until evenly finely chopped. Remove to a bowl and rinse out Pitcher.
2. Place onion and garlic powder pieces in the Pitcher. PULSE until the onion and garlic powder are finely chopped. Add to potatoes and beetroots.
3. Add coconut flour, eggs, salt and pepper to the potato mixture and gently combine, being sure not to over mix.
4. Set Ninja Cooking System to STOVETOP HIGH. Add coconut oil to pot. Spoon 1/8 cup potato mixture into oil and flatten to 3–inch diameter with spatula. Cook until golden brown, about 1 1/2 minutes on each side. Place cooked latkes on paper towels to drain.

Nutrition Facts

Calories 213, Total Fat 9.5g, Saturated Fat 6.9g, Cholesterol 82mg, Sodium 377mg, Total Carbohydrate 27.4g, Dietary Fiber 5g, Total Sugars 7.2g, Protein 6.3g

Pomegranates and Cheese Pinwheels

(Prep Time: 15 min |Cooking Time: 15 min | serve: 2)

Ingredients

- ¼ cup Pomegranates
- ¼ cup goat cheese
- ¼ cup heavy cream
- ¼ cup crumbled mozzarella cheese
- 1/8 cup chopped green onion
- 2 large flour kale tortillas

Preparation

1. Place Ingredients, except tortillas, into the blender and pulse 4-5 times.
2. Spoon the mixture onto the tortillas and spread evenly, and then roll up the tortillas tightly, wrap in plastic and then refrigerate for at least an hour.
3. Slice into 1-2 inch pieces.

Nutrition Facts

Calories 145, Total Fat 8.1g, Saturated Fat 4.8g, Cholesterol 26mg, Sodium 51mg, Total Carbohydrate 15.1g, Dietary Fiber 1.8g, Total Sugars 3.1g, Protein 4g

Chapter 8 Desserts

Key Lime Pie

(Prep Time: 15 min |Cooking Time: 00 min | serve: 2)

Ingredients

- 3 Oreo cookies
- 1 tablespoon coconut oil
- ½ cup cream cheese, softened
- 1/8 cup honey
- ¼ cup lime juice
- 1 tablespoon coconut milk
- ¼ cup + 1 tablespoons coconut cream
- ¼ cup heavy whipping cream

Preparation

1. Place the Total Crushing & Power Chopping Blade into the Jar, then add Oreo cookies
2. Pulse 7 times. Add melted coconut oil and pulse 3 times.
3. Transfer mixture to a 9-inch circular pie pan. Using your hands, press mixture evenly into the pan to form a crust. Place uncovered in the refrigerator.
4. Place the High-Speed Blade into the Jar, then add cream cheese, honey, lime juice, coconut milk, and coconut cream.
5. Pulse 3 times, then run continuously for 30 seconds or until desired consistency is achieved. Transfer to a medium bowl and set aside.
6. Wash the jar and High-Speed Blade. Place High-Speed Blade back into jar, then add the heavy whipping cream. Run continuously for 10 seconds.
7. Using a spatula, gently fold the whipped cream into the cream cheese mixture.
8. Remove the Oreo cookies crust from the refrigerator. Pour mixture over the crust.
9. Using a spatula, gently spread mixture evenly across the crust.
10. Place back into the refrigerator and chill for a minimum of 8 hours.

Nutrition Facts

Calories 598, Total Fat 43.3g, Saturated Fat 29.9g, Cholesterol 84mg, Sodium 265mg, Total Carbohydrate 50.7g, Dietary Fiber 0.8g, Total Sugars 43g, Protein 6.2g

Figs Bites

(Prep Time: 05 min |Cooking Time: 00 min | serve: 2)

Ingredients

- 1 cup figs
- ¼ cup raw cashew
- ¼ cup quinoa
- 1tablespoon almond butter
- 1 tablespoon ground coffee
- 1/8 teaspoon kosher salt
- 1/4 cup shredded toasted coconut

Preparation

1. Place Total Crushing & Power Chopping Blade into the Jar, then add all Ingredients in the order listed.
2. Pulse 10 to 12 times or until desired consistency is achieved.
3. Using a 1-inch ice cream scoop or your hands, form the mixture into balls

Nutrition Facts

Calories 254, Total Fat 9g, Saturated Fat 2.6g, Cholesterol 0mg, Sodium 82mg, Total Carbohydrate 42.9g, Dietary Fiber 6.7g, Total Sugars 24.8g, Protein 5.5g

Pound Cake

(Prep Time: 10 min |Cooking Time: 25 min | serve: 2)

Ingredients

- ½ cup coconut oil
- ½ cup maple syrup
- 2 large eggs room temp
- 1 teaspoon Vanilla Extract
- 1 cup coconut flour
- ½ orange zest only

Preparation

1. Using a stand mixer, combine the butter and the maple syrup and beat using the paddle attachment until the mixture is light and fluffy. Scraping down the sides every few minutes.
2. Add one egg at a time and beat on low until incorporated. Repeat with remaining one egg.
3. Add in vanilla extract and mix just to incorporate.
4. Slowly add coconut flour and mix in stand mixer. Mix on low just until all the flour is incorporated, don't over mix.
5. Add the zest from orange and stir to incorporate.
6. Butter 7" Ring Mold pan. Put 2 cups of water in the inner pot of the Ninja Foodi. Cover the cake with foil and tent it just a bit. Put on the rack in the low position in the Ninja Foodi. Set pressure on high for 25 minutes. Make sure the black valve is in the seal position. When the time is up, allow to natural release for 20 minutes.
7. When the natural release is up, manual release any pressure. There might not be any and the red pin may already be depressed. Set on cooling rack and cool for 5 minutes.
8. Invert cake onto cooling rack and gently place the cake back on the rack in the low position. Return the cake to the Ninja Foodi. Set the Bake/Roast function to 400°F and bake 5-10 minutes or until the top is golden brown.
9. Remove and allow to cool on the rack for about an hour. Serve & Enjoy!

Nutrition Facts

Calories 373, Total Fat 27.9g, Saturated Fat 24.1g, Cholesterol 0mg, Sodium 28mg, Total Carbohydrate 30.9g, Dietary Fiber 1.6g, Total Sugars 25.4g,Protein 2.5g

Beetroots Peaches Cake Bites

(Prep Time: 15 min |Cooking Time: 00 min | serve: 2)

Ingredients

- 1 dates
- 1/8 cup banana
- 1/8 cup all-purpose flour
- 1 teaspoon vanilla extract
- 1/4 teaspoon ground nutmeg
- 1/8 teaspoon ground cardamom
- 1/8 teaspoon ground ginger
- 1 cup shredded beetroots
- Unsweetened shredded coconut, for garnish
- 1/8 teaspoon ground cinnamon
- 2 peaches

Preparation

1. Place all Ingredients, except shredded coconut, into the Nutri Bow in the order listed.
2. Select Auto-iQ BOOST™ YES FUSION MIX.
3. Roll dough into 18 evenly sized bites, about 1 inch round. Roll each bite in shredded coconut.
4. Refrigerate for 1 hour before serving.

Nutrition Facts

Calories 124, Total Fat 4.7g, Saturated Fat 3.8g, Cholesterol 0mg, Sodium 48mg, Total Carbohydrate 19.2g, Dietary Fiber 3.5g, Total Sugars 13g, Protein 2.4g

Zeppole

(Prep Time: 30 min |Cooking Time: 20 min | serve: 2)

Ingredients

- ¼ tablespoon water
- 1/8 teaspoon active dry yeast
- 1 tablespoons honey
- ½ cup coconut flour
- 1/8 cup goat cheese
- 1 large egg
- Zest of 1 lemon
- 1/8 teaspoon vanilla extract
- 1/8 teaspoon kosher salt
- 1/8 teaspoon cinnamon
- 1 tablespoon coconut oil

Preparation

1. Warm water to 110° F, then combine with yeast and ¼ teaspoon honey in the bowl of a stand mixer and let sit until mixture becomes foamy, about 5 minutes.
2. Add coconut flour, goat, egg, lemon zest, vanilla, salt, cinnamon, and remaining ½ tablespoons honey, and attach bowl to stand mixer fitted with dough hook attachment. Mix on low speed until the dough forms.
3. Gradually add 1/2 tablespoon coconut oil , one tablespoon at a time, occasionally stopping mixer to scrape down sides of bowl. Increase speed to medium and beat until dough is cohesive, smooth, and glossy, about 4 minutes. If necessary, scrape dough from hook and sides of bowl. Remove bowl from mixer, cover with plastic wrap and let rise at room temperate for 2 hours.
4. Transfer dough to a lightly floured surface and shape into a smooth ball. Divide into 6 equal portions and roll into tight balls. Place on a baking sheet and let sit covered at room temperature for 30 minutes.
5. After 30 minutes, close crisping lid. Preheat the unit by selecting AIR CRISP, setting the temperature to 360°F, and setting the time to 3 minutes. Select START/STOP to begin.
6. Melt remaining ¼ tablespoon coconut oil. Brush half the dough balls with melted butter and place them in the Cook & Crisp™ Basket. Reserve unused butter.
7. Once unit has preheated, place basket in pot. Close lid. Select AIR CRISP, set temperature to 360°F, and set time to 12 minutes. Select START/STOP to begin.
8. Cooking is complete when zeppole are deep golden brown. Remove them from basket, brush again with melted oil,
9. Repeat steps 6 through 8 with remaining dough balls. Serve warm.

Nutrition Facts

Calories 76, Total Fat 5.2g, Saturated Fat 3.8g, Cholesterol 47mg, Sodium 98mg, Total Carbohydrate 5.7g, Dietary Fiber 0.8g, Total Sugars 4.6g, Protein 2.2g

Pears Foster

(Prep Time: 05 min |Cooking Time: 05 min | serve: 2)

Ingredients

- ¼ cup coconut oil
- ½ cup honey
- ½ teaspoon ground nutmeg
- 2 small pears, peeled, cut half lengthwise, then cut in half again
- ¼ cup rum
- Chocolate ice cream, for serving

Preparation

1. Select SEAR/SAUTÉ and set to MD:HI. Select START/STOP to begin. Allow to preheat for 5 minutes.
2. After 5 minutes, place coconut oil, honey, and nutmeg in the pot. Stir until coconut oil and honey mix well.
3. Add pears to pot. Spoon the sauce over them and cook until their edges start to soften and mixture begins to bubble.
4. Stir in the rum. Cook for another 2 minutes.
5. Select START/STOP to turn off unit. Serve bananas immediately with chocolate ice cream.

Nutrition Facts

Calories 245, Total Fat 5.4g, Saturated Fat 3.7g, Cholesterol 15mg, Sodium 29mg, Total Carbohydrate 34g, Dietary Fiber 4.9g, Total Sugars 24.9g, Protein 1.7g

Flax Seeds Cashew Bites

(Prep Time: 20 min |Cooking Time: 00 min | serve: 2)

Ingredients

- 1 tablespoon cashews
- 1 tablespoon dark chocolate chips
- 1 date, cut in half, pits removed
- 1 teaspoon butter, melted
- ½ tablespoon peanut butter
- 1 teaspoon flex seeds
- ¼ cup quinoa flakes

Preparation

1. Place all Ingredients into the Food Processor in the order listed.
2. Select HIGH until mixture is well combined.
3. Roll dough into 6 evenly sized bites, about 1 1/4 inches round. Refrigerate 1 hour before serving.

Nutrition Facts

Calories 74, Total Fat 4g, Saturated Fat 1.3g, Cholesterol 3mg, Sodium 17mg, Total Carbohydrate 8.5g, Dietary Fiber 1g, Total Sugars 3g, Protein 2g

Peaches Bundt Cake

(Prep Time: 20 min |Cooking Time:60 min | serve: 2)

Ingredients

- 4 peaches, peeled, cored, diced
- 2 large eggs
- 1 cup + 4 teaspoons honey, divided
- 1/2 cup coconut oil
- 1/3 cup lemon juice
- 2 teaspoons vanilla extract
- 2 cups coconut flour
- 1 teaspoon baking powder
- 1/4 teaspoon salt
- 2 teaspoons ground nutmeg

Preparation

1. Preheat oven to 350°F. Grease a Bundt pan with cooking spray; set aside.
2. Place the double dough hook in the 40-ounce Blend & Prep Bowl and add peaches, eggs, 1 cup honey, coconut oil, lemon juice, and vanilla extract. Select START/STOP until Ingredients are well mixed.
3. Add coconut flour, baking powder, salt, and nutmeg, and select LOW until combined, scraping down sides of bowl as needed.
4. Pour batter into the prepared Bundt pan and bake for approximately 1 hour or until a wooden toothpick inserted in cake comes out clean.

Nutrition Facts

Calories 394, Total Fat 31.7g, Saturated Fat 25.8g, Cholesterol 93mg, Sodium 203mg, Total Carbohydrate 24.4g, Dietary Fiber 5.2g, Total Sugars 20g, Protein 5.8g

Squash Cupcakes

(Prep Time: 10 min |Cooking Time: 25 min | serve: 2)

Ingredients

- 1 cup squash, peeled and cut into 3-inch pieces
- 1 tablespoon coconut oil
- ¼ cup maple syrup
- ¼ teaspoon vanilla extract
- ½ cup almond flour
- ¼ teaspoon baking soda
- ¼ teaspoon baking powder
- 1/8 teaspoon salt
- 1/8 teaspoon ground nutmeg

Preparation

1. Preheat the oven to 350°F. Line a 4-cup cupcake pan with paper liners; set aside. Place the shredder disc onto the spindle in the bowl and attach the lid. Select Speed 1. Using the food pusher, push the carrots through the feed chute.
2. Remove the shredded squash and place into a large mixing bowl; set aside. Using the dough attachment in the 64-ounce Food Processor bowl, add the remaining Ingredients in the order listed, starting with vegetable oil.
3. Process on Speed 1 for 15 to 20 seconds or until all Ingredients are fully combined. Batter will be really thick. Add batter into the mixing bowl with the squash. Fold in all the squash with a spatula.
4. Pour mixture into the cupcake molds. Bake 20 to 25 minutes, or until a toothpick inserted into the centre of the cupcakes comes out clean. Let cool in pan for 20 minutes, then remove and cool completely on a wire rack.

Nutrition Facts

Calories 167, Total Fat 10.5g, Saturated Fat 3.5g, Cholesterol 0mg, Sodium 158mg, Total Carbohydrate 17.4g, Dietary Fiber 1.8g, Total Sugars 12.8g, Protein 3.3g

Pears Pie

(Prep Time: 10 min |Cooking Time: 40 min | serve: 2)

Ingredients

- 6 pears, peeled, cored and thinly sliced
- ½ cup currants
- 2 teaspoons orange zest
- 2 tablespoons orange juice
- 1 vanilla bean, split
- 1 teaspoon ground nutmeg
- 1 teaspoon ground cardamom
- ½ cup maple syrup
- 3 tablespoons almond flour
- 3 tablespoons coconut oil

Preparation

1. On lightly floured work surface, roll one-half of pie dough into an 11-inch circle. Arrange crust in 9-inch glass pie pan and trim excess edges with knife.
2. Preheat oven to 400 °F. In a large bowl toss pears and sultanas with orange zest and orange juice. Set aside.
3. Place the dough attachment in the Bowl. Blend the vanilla bean scraping, nutmeg, cardamom, honey and flour on 1, mixing well to combine. Add butter and blend again on 1 until crumbly. Add the mixture to the pears slices and toss well to combine.
4. Mound pears mixture into pie pan. Roll out remaining pie dough into an 11-inch circle and arrange on top of pears. Crimp edges to seal and cut slits to vent steam.
5. Bake for 35 to 40 minutes until apples are tender and crust is golden. Let set for 10 minutes before serving.

Nutrition Facts

Calories 306, Total Fat 12.7g, Saturated Fat 9.1g, Cholesterol 0mg, Sodium 4mg, Total Carbohydrate 52.1g, Dietary Fiber 11.1g, Total Sugars 32.5g, Protein 2.2g

Chapter 9 Side Dishes

Sweet Potatoes Fries

(Prep Time: 15 min |Cooking Time: 15 min.| serve: 2)

Ingredients

- ¼ cup water
- 2 Sweet potatoes, cut in 2-inch wedges
- 1 tablespoon coconut oil, divided
- ½ tablespoon fresh basil leaves, minced
- 1 teaspoon garlic powder
- Juice of 1 lime
- 1 teaspoon kosher salt
- ½ teaspoon ground black pepper

Preparation

1. Pour water into the pot. Place Sweet potatoes into the Cook & Crisp Basket and place basket into pot.
2. Assemble pressure lid, making sure the PRESSURE RELEASE valve is in the SEAL position. Select PRESSURE and set to LOW. Set time to 3 minutes. Select START/STOP to begin.
3. While potatoes are cooking, stir together ½ tablespoon coconut oil with basil, garlic powder, lime juice, salt, and pepper in a small bowl. Set aside.
4. When pressure cooking is complete, quick release the pressure by moving the PRESSURE RELEASE valve to the VENT position. Carefully remove lid when unit has finished releasing pressure.
5. Pour remaining coconut oil over the Sweet potatoes in the basket, shaking to coat evenly.
6. Close the crisping lid. Select AIR CRISP, set temperature to 400°F, and set time to 18 minutes. Select START/STOP to begin. Check Sweet potatoes after 12 minutes. Continue cooking for up to 18 minutes for desired crispiness.
7. When cooking is complete, remove Sweet potatoes from basket. Toss with oregano dressing and serve.

Nutrition Facts

Calories 247, Total Fat 7.1g, Saturated Fat 6g, Cholesterol 0mg, Sodium 1178mg, Total Carbohydrate 45.1g, Dietary Fiber 6.5g, Total Sugars 1.5g, Protein 2.7g

Squash Fries with Marinara Sauce

(Prep Time: 50 min |Cooking Time: 20 min.| serve: 2)

Ingredients

- 1 large squash, cut in sticks 3-inches long and 1/4-inch thick
- 1 teaspoon salt
- 1cup coconut flour
- 2 eggs, beaten
- 1-1/2 cups panko bread crumbs
- 1/8 cup grated goat cheese
- ½ tablespoon garlic minced
- 1 teaspoons onion powder
- Marinara sauce, for serving

Preparation

1. Place the squash sticks onto a plate and sprinkle with salt. Allow to sit at room temperature for 15 minutes to remove excess liquid. Pat dry.
2. Place coconut flour into a bowl. Place beaten eggs in another bowl. Combine panko bread crumbs, goat, garlic, and onion powder in a third bowl.
3. First, dredge fries in the coconut flour, then shake off any excess and coat in the egg. Then coat in panko bread crumb mixture and return to a clean plate. Repeat with remaining squash. Cover plate with plastic wrap and place in the freezer for 30 to 45 minutes.
4. Once coating has hardened, place the Cook & Cris Basket in the pot. Close crisping lid. Preheat the unit by selecting AIR CRISP, setting the temperature to 360°F, and setting the time to 5 minutes. Press START/STOP to begin.
5. After 5 minutes, open lid and add zucchini fries to basket. Close lid. Select AIR CRISP, set temperature to 360°F, and set time to 24 minutes. Press START/STOP to begin.
6. After 12 minutes, open lid, then lift basket and shake Squash fries or toss them with silicone-tipped tongs. Lower basket back into pot and close lid to resume cooking.
7. After 20 minutes, check fries for desired doneness. Cook for up to 5 more minutes for crispier results. When cooking is complete, serve fries immediately with marinara sauce.

Nutrition Facts

Calories 402, Total Fat 10.9g, Saturated Fat 4g, Cholesterol 167mg, Sodium 1914mg, Total Carbohydrate 58.9g, Dietary Fiber 8.5g, Total Sugars 13g, Protein 17.6g

Crispy Broccoli

(Prep Time: 05 min |Cooking Time: 15 min.| serve: 2)

Ingredients

- 1 cup broccoli
- 1 tablespoon butter
- ½ teaspoon salt
- ¼ teaspoon ground black pepper

Preparation

1. Place Cook & Crisp Basket in pot. Close crisping lid. Preheat the unit by selecting AIR CRISP, setting the temperature to 390°F, and setting the time to 5 minutes.
2. Meanwhile, in a bowl, toss broccoli with melted butter, salt, and pepper.
3. After 5 minutes, add broccoli to basket. Close crisping lid. Select AIR CRISP, set temperature to 390°F, and set time to 12 minutes. Select START/STOP to begin.
4. After 6 minutes, open lid, then lift basket and shake broccoli or toss them with silicone-tipped tongs. Lower basket back into pot and close lid to resume cooking.
5. Check broccoli for desired doneness; for crispier results, add up to 3 more minutes. When cooking is complete, remove Brussels sprouts from basket.

Nutrition Facts

Calories 67, Total Fat 5.9g, Saturated Fat 3.7g, Cholesterol 15mg, Sodium 637mg, Total Carbohydrate 3.2g, Dietary Fiber 1.3g, Total Sugars 0.8g, Protein 1.4g

Greens Sauté

(Prep Time: 15 min |Cooking Time: 12 min.| serve: 2)

Ingredients

- 1 tablespoon coconut oil
- ¼ cup crumbled tofu
- 1 small onion, peeled, sliced
- 1 bunch Kale stems removed, cleaned, sliced in 1/4-inch ribbons
- ¼ cup low-sodium vegetable stock
- ¼ cup white wine vinegar
- ½ teaspoon red pepper flakes
- 1 teaspoons salt

Preparation

1. Select SEAR/SAUTÉ and set to HIGH. Select START/STOP to begin. Allow to preheat for 5 minutes.
2. After 5 minutes, add coconut oil, and onion to the pot. Cook for 8 minutes, or until pancetta is rendered and onions begin to caramelize.
3. Add kale, broth, white wine vinegar, red pepper flakes, and salt to the pot. Stir to incorporate.
4. Assemble pressure lid, making sure the pressure release valve is in the SEAL position.
5. Select PRESSURE and set to HIGH. Set time to 4 minutes. Select START/STOP to begin.
6. When pressure cooking is complete, allow pressure to natural release for 10 minutes. After 10 minutes, quick release remaining pressure by moving the pressure release valve to the VENT position. Carefully remove lid when unit has finished releasing pressure.

Nutrition Facts

Calories 120, Total Fat 8.5g, Saturated Fat 6.4g, Cholesterol 0mg, Sodium 1274mg, Total Carbohydrate 8.1g, Dietary Fiber 1.7g, Total Sugars 2.1g, Protein 4g

Crispy Peanuts

(Prep Time: 05 min |Cooking Time: 20 min.| serve: 2)

Ingredients

- 1 cup peanuts
- 1 tablespoon coconut oil, divided
- ½ teaspoon kosher salt, plus more for seasoning
- 1 tablespoon honey
- 1 teaspoon nutmeg

Preparation

1. Select SEAR/SAUTÉ and set to HIGH. Select START/STOP to begin. Allow to preheat for 3 minutes.
2. After 3 minutes, add peanuts to the pot. Sauté until they begin turning golden in spots, about 5 minutes.
3. Toss peanuts with remaining oil and desired seasonings, then transfer to the Cook & Crisp™ Basket. Place basket in pot.
4. Close the crisping lid. Select AIR CRISP, set temperature to 400°F, and set time to 15 minutes, stirring halfway through.
5. When cooking is complete, carefully transfer peanuts to a serving bowl. Serve immediately.

Nutrition Facts

Calories 303, Total Fat 25.2g, Saturated Fat 8.7g, Cholesterol 0mg, Sodium 589mg, Total Carbohydrate 15.1g,Dietary Fiber 3.4g, Total Sugars 10.4g, Protein 9.5g

Milton Keynes UK
Ingram Content Group UK Ltd.
UKHW051005141123
432477UK00023B/703

9 781637 331231